This workbook belongs

MW01131799

Hello 你好 nǐ hǎo

Chinese For Kids Workbook: Kindergarten uses a step-by-step approach to help children learn Mandarin Chinese with writing exercises. Engaging activities allow parents and children to stay motivated as they learn together.

Each topic and activity has simplified characters with Pinyin and English translations. Chinese is not a spelling language. Learning to memorize characters without Pinyin and English translations next to them is an important skill. To encourage your child to recognize characters, the review activity page at the end of each topic does not have Pinyin and English translations. We have included extra writing pages and answer keys to help children practice the characters. Thank you for choosing this workbook in your learning journey!

How to Trace:
Trace over the gray strokes by following the correct numbered stroke diagram. Do not worry about the thickness of the gray lines. Use a pencil or pen to trace down the middle of the gray lines. Practice with this sample grid.

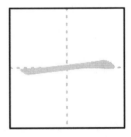

Chinese For Kids Workbook
Kindergarten
Copyright 2019 Queenie Law
www.adoreneko.com
ISBN: 9781696812849

Contents

Basic Writing Strokes 1

Compound Writing Strokes 11

Opposites 18

Numbers 1–10 26

Math Concepts 39

Measure Words 42

Chinese Culture 52

Checklist 54

Writing Practice 55

Answer Key 102

Let's Learn Basic Writing Strokes

 All Chinese characters are written with strokes. The same stroke may be written in more than one way. Let's learn some basic writing strokes.

Basic Strokes	Stroke Name	
丷 ⺀	点	dot diǎn
一 一	横	horizontal héng
丨 丨	竖	vertical shù
丿 丿 ⼂ ⼃	撇	falling piě
乀 乀	捺	down nà
⼂ ⼃ ⼃	提	rise tí
亅 亅	钩	hook gōu
㇇ ㇆ ㇆	折	break zhé

Start writing a basic stroke from the top, left or right. Rise (tí) is the only stroke that begins from the bottom.

Trace and write each 点 dot (diǎn) stroke.

 Color each diǎn stroke.

WORD

word	inch	fire
zì	cùn	huǒ

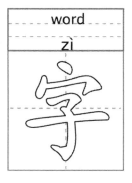

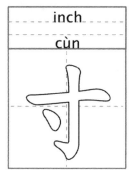

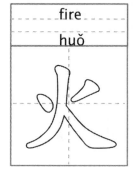

 Write the missing diǎn stroke(s).

word (zì)   inch (cùn)   fire (huǒ)

2

Trace and write each 横 horizontal (héng) stroke.

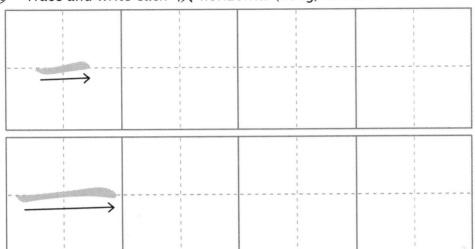

 Color each héng stroke.

king
wáng

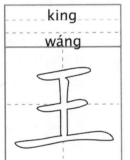

sky, day
tiān

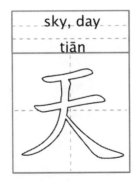

three
sān

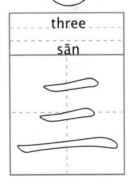

 Write the missing héng stroke(s).

king (wáng)

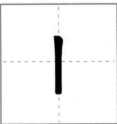

day, sky (tiān)

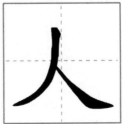

three (sān)

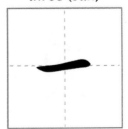

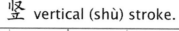

✏️ Trace and write each 竖 vertical (shù) stroke.

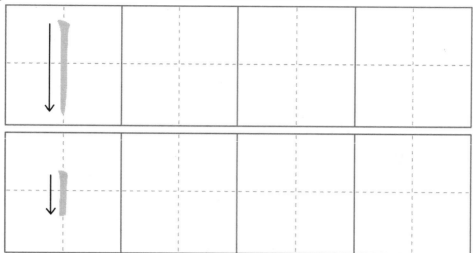

🖍️ Color each shù stroke.

work	ten	up
gōng	shí	shàng

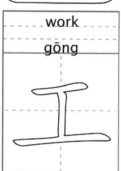

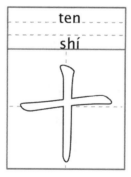

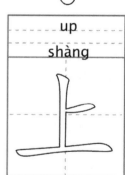

✏️ Write the missing shù stroke(s).

work (gōng)	ten (shí)	up (shàng)

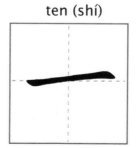
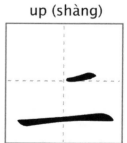

Trace and write each 撇 falling (piě) stroke.

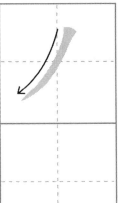 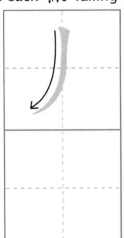 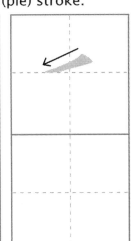 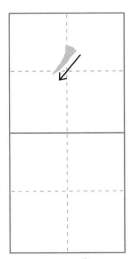

 Color each piě stroke.

knife	big	hand	cow
dāo	dà	shǒu	niú

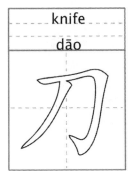 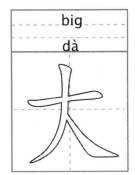  

 Write the missing piě stroke(s).

knife (dāo)　　　big (dà)　　　hand (shǒu)　　　cow (niú)

 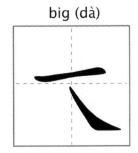  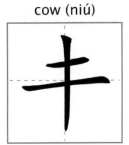

Trace and write the 捺 down (nà) stroke.

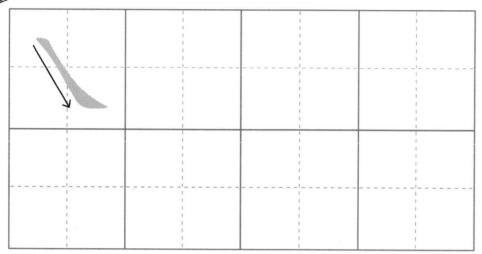

 Color each nà stroke.

eight	person	fork
bā	rén	chā

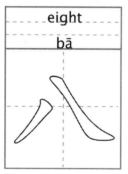

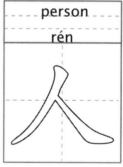

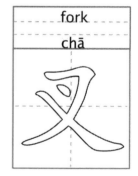

 Write the missing nà stroke(s).

eight (bā)   person (rén)   fork (chā)

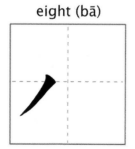

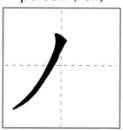

✏️ Trace and write each 提 rise (tí) stroke.

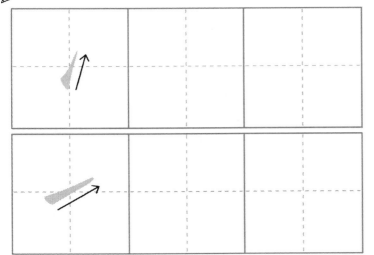

Tip

Tí is the only Chinese stroke written upwards and to the right.

🖍️ Color each tí stroke.

juice
zhī

ice
bīng

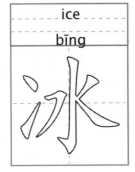

I, me
wǒ

✏️ Write the missing tí stroke(s).

juice (zhī)	ice (bīng)	I, me (wǒ)

Trace and write the 钩 hook (gōu) stroke.

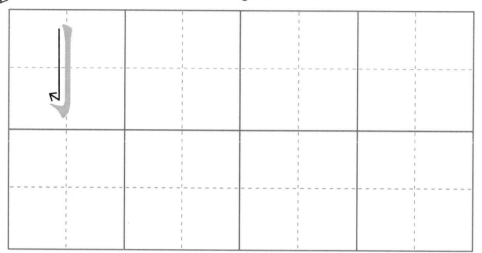

 Color each gōu stroke.

| water |
| shuǐ |

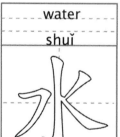

| small |
| xiǎo |

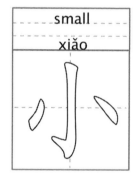

| inch |
| cùn |

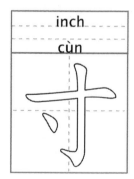

 Write the missing gōu stroke(s).

water (shuǐ)   small (xiǎo)   inch (cùn)

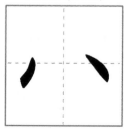

Trace and write the 折 break (zhé) stroke.

 Color each zhé stroke.

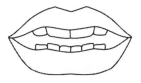

mouth	five	shell
kǒu	wǔ	bèi

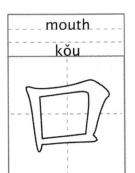

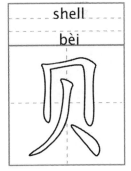

 Write the missing zhé stroke(s).

mouth (kǒu)   five (wǔ)   shell (bèi)

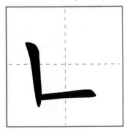

9

Let's Review Basic Writing Strokes

 Draw a line from each stroke to complete the word.

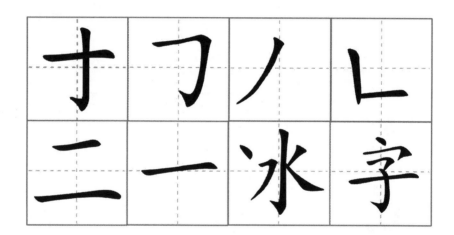

  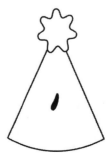 

Let's Learn Compound Writing Strokes

 Compound strokes are a combination of 2 or more basic strokes. Let's learn some compound writing strokes.

Compound Strokes	Stroke Name	
㇄	竖折	vertical break shù zhé
㇆	横钩	horizontal hook héng gōu
㇇	横撇	héng piě horizontal left falling
㇌	横折弯钩	horizontal break bend hook héng zhé wān gōu
㇉	竖弯钩	shù wān gōu vertical bend hook

All compound strokes are written starting from the top, left or right.

Trace and write the 竖折 vertical break (shù zhé) stroke.

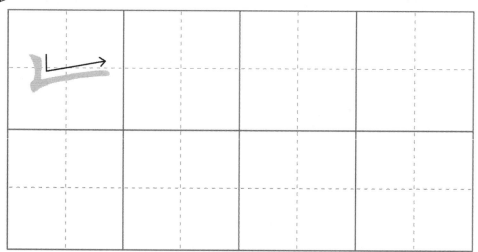

 Color each shù zhé stroke.

| mountain |
| shān |

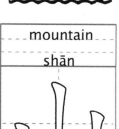

| go out |
| chū |

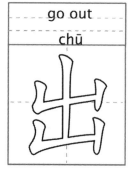

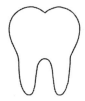

| tooth |
| yá |

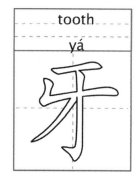

 Write the missing shù zhé stroke(s).

| mountain (shān) | go out (chū) | tooth (yá) |

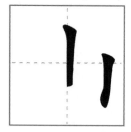

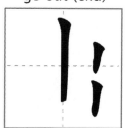

Trace and write the 横钩 horizontal hook (héng gōu) stroke.

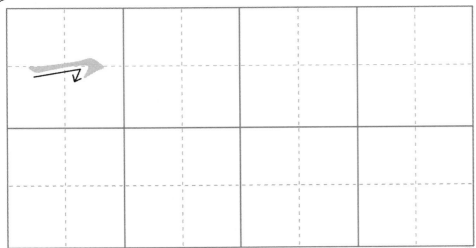

 Color each héng gōu stroke.

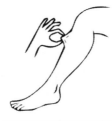

buy	skin	word
mǎi	pí	zì

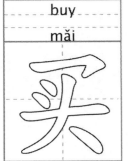

 Write the missing héng gōu stroke(s).

buy (mǎi)   skin (pí)   word (zì)

13

Trace and write the 横撇 horizontal left falling (héng piě) stroke.

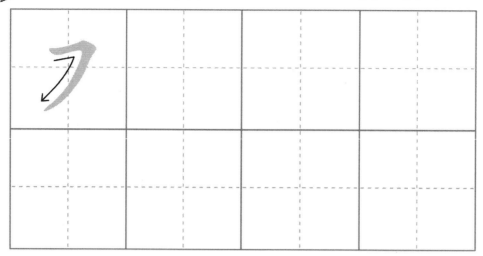

 Color each héng piě stroke.

| fork |
| chā |

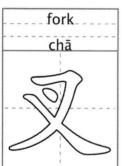

| many |
| duō |

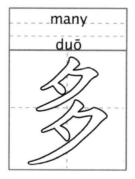

| water |
| shuǐ |

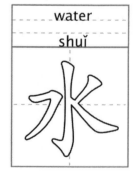

 Write the missing héng piě stroke(s).

fork (chā)   many (duō)   water (shuǐ)

   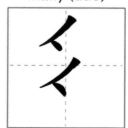   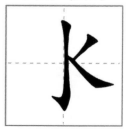

14

✏️ Trace and write the 横折弯钩 horizontal break bend hook (héng zhé wān gōu) stroke.

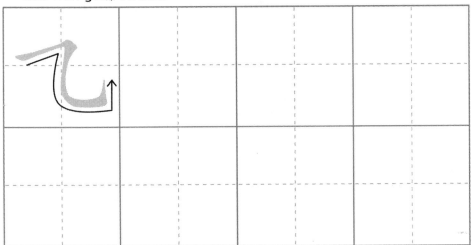

🖍️ Color each héng zhé wān gōu stroke.

nine
jiǔ

eat
chī

pill
wán

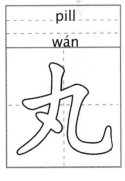

✏️ Write the missing héng zhé wān gōu stroke(s).

nine (jiǔ)

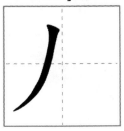

eat (chī)

pill (wán)

Trace and write the 竖弯钩 vertical bend hook (shù wān gōu) stroke.

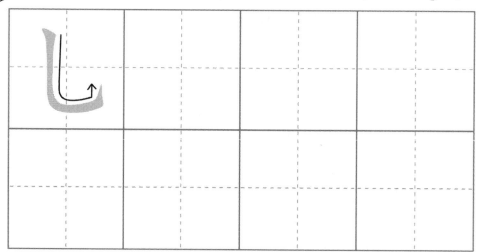

 Color each shù wān gōu stroke.

seven	dragon	pond
qī	lóng	chí

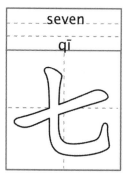

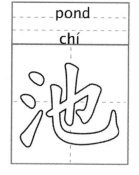

 Write the missing shù wān gōu stroke(s).

seven (qī)	dragon (lóng)	pond (chí)

16

Let's Review Compound Writing Strokes

✏️ Draw a line from each stroke to complete the word.

Let's Learn Opposites

Learning opposite words together will help you remember Chinese characters. Let's learn some opposite words in Chinese.

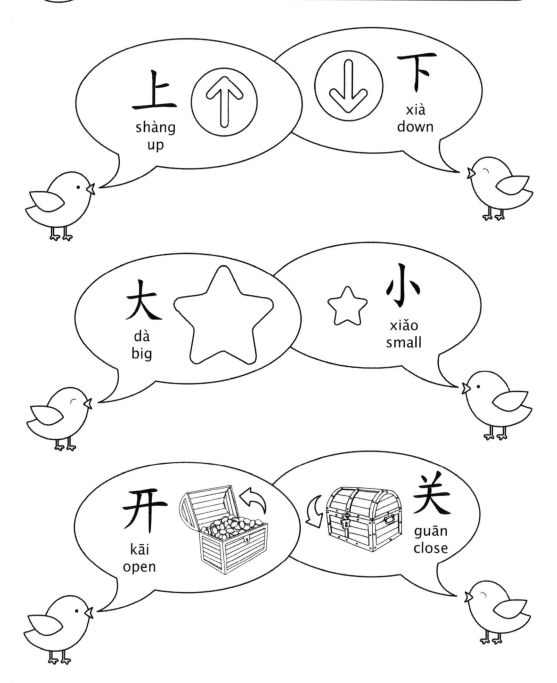

上
shàng
up

下
xià
down

大
dà
big

小
xiǎo
small

开
kāi
open

关
guān
close

Trace each stroke.

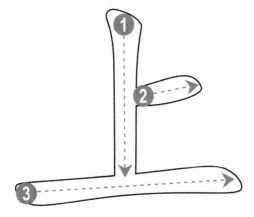

shàng
up

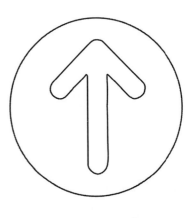

 Trace and write.

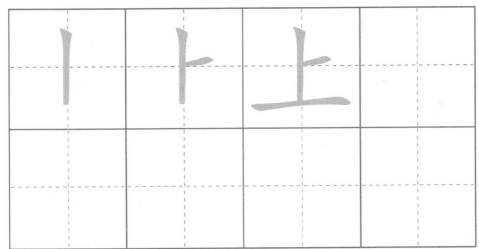

 Color the picture that shows 上.

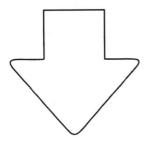 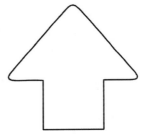

Trace each stroke.

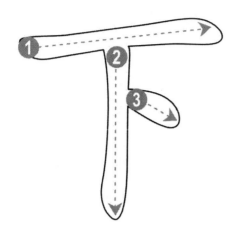

xià
down

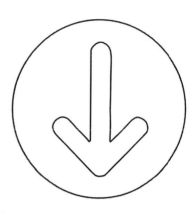

 Trace and write.

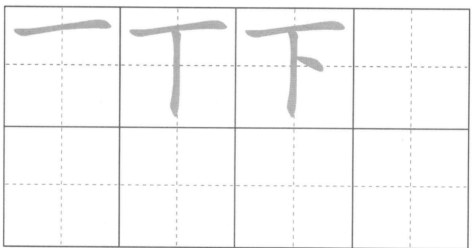

 Color the picture that shows 下 .

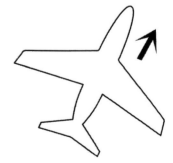

Trace each stroke.

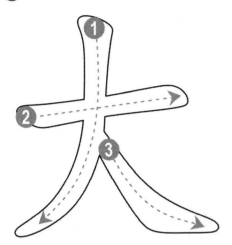

dà
big

 Trace and write.

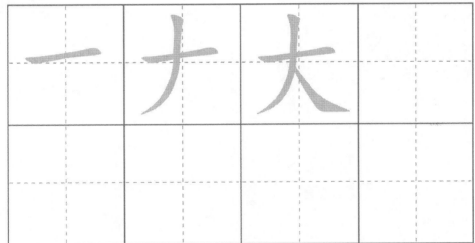

 Color the picture that shows 大 .

Trace each stroke.

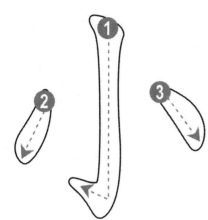

xiǎo
small

 Trace and write.

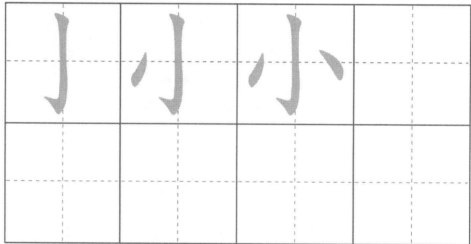

 Color the picture that shows 小 .

Trace each stroke.

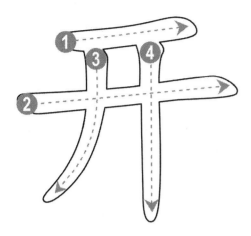

kāi
open

 Trace and write.

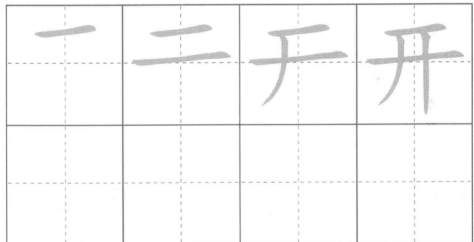

 Color the picture that shows 开.

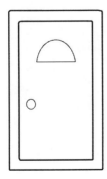

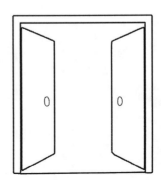

Trace each stroke.

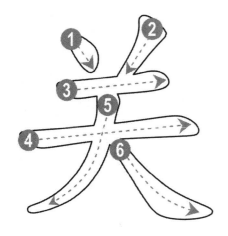

guān
close

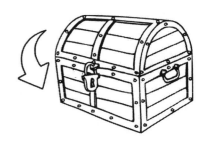

 Trace and write.

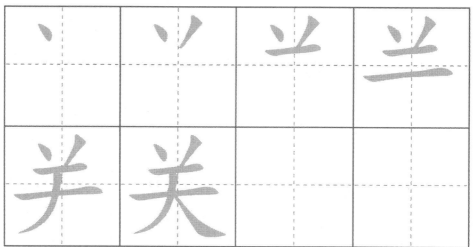

 Color the picture that shows 关.

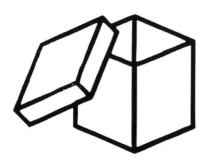

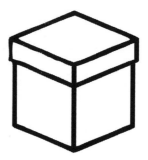

Let's Review Opposites

 Draw lines to match the opposite words.

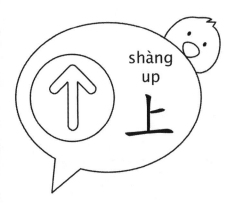

shàng
up

上

guān
close

关

dà
big

大

xià
down

下

kāi
open

开

xiǎo
small

小

Let's Learn Numbers 1-10

 Chinese numbers from 1 to 10 are simple, one syllable words. Let's look at Chinese numbers 1 to 10.

Character	Pinyin	Number
一	yī	1
二	èr	2
三	sān	3
四	sì	4
五	wǔ	5
六	liù	6
七	qī	7
八	bā	8
九	jiǔ	9
十	shí	10

Pencil Control ✏ Trace the gray shapes below to draw a fish.

1. Draw a triangle   2. Draw an oval.   3. Add a dot for an eye.

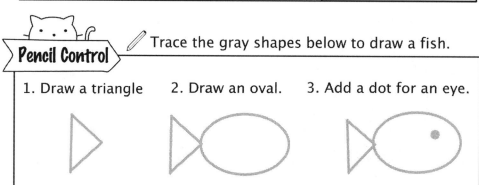

👆 Trace the 一 .

一 ☆
yī
one

1

✏️ Trace and write 一 .

✏️ Draw 一 fish.

27

Trace the 二 .

① ➡
② ➡

èr
two

2

Trace and write 二 .

一	二		

Draw 二 fish.

28

👆 Trace the 三 .

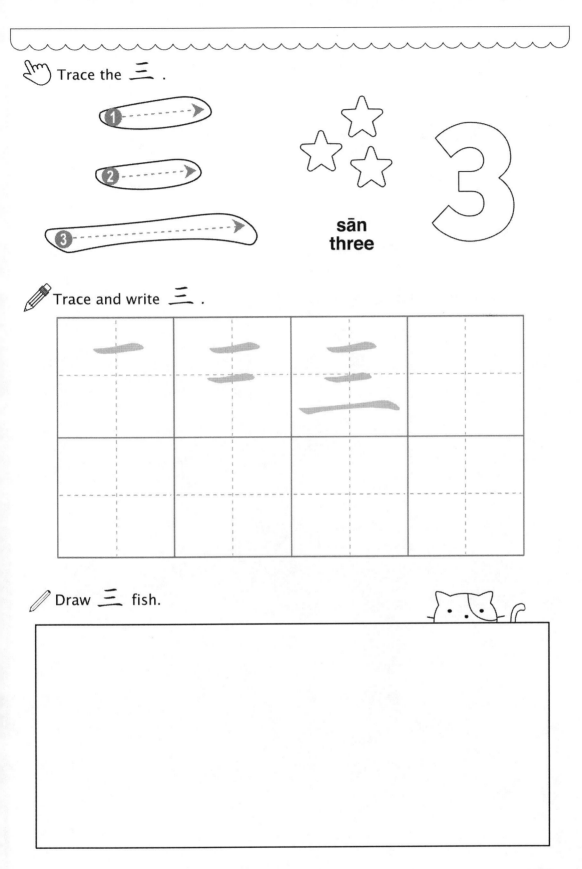

sān
three

✏️ Trace and write 三 .

✏️ Draw 三 fish.

👆 Trace the 四.

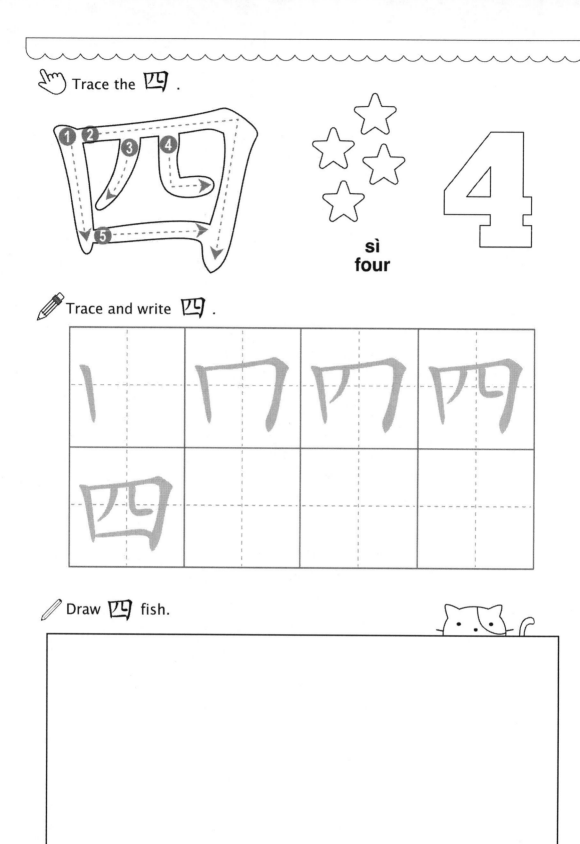

sì
four

4

✏️ Trace and write 四.

丨	冂	冂	四
四			

✏️ Draw 四 fish.

👆 Trace the 五 .

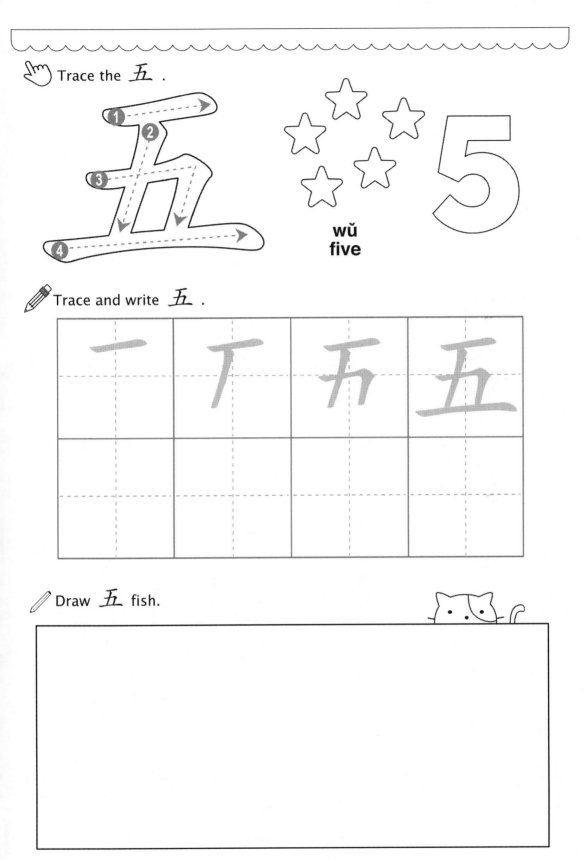

wǔ
five

✏️ Trace and write 五 .

一	丆	玊	五

✏️ Draw 五 fish.

Trace the 六 .

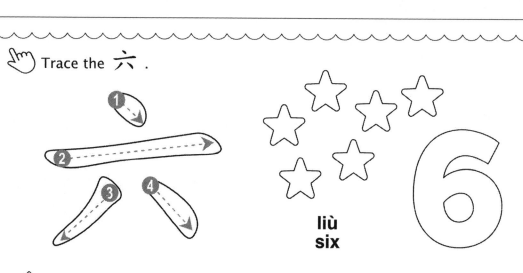

liù
six

Trace and write 六 .

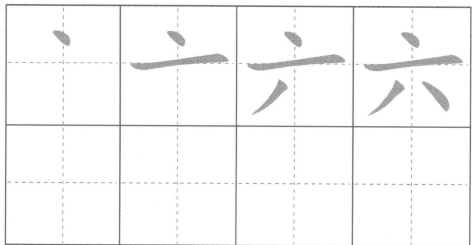

Color 六 squares of fish.

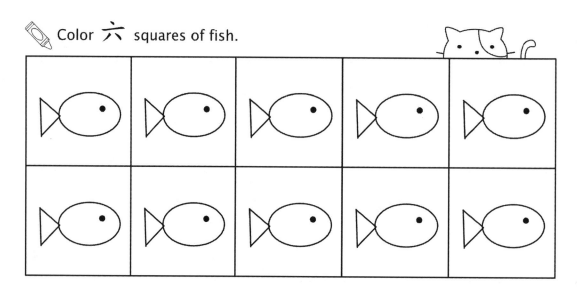

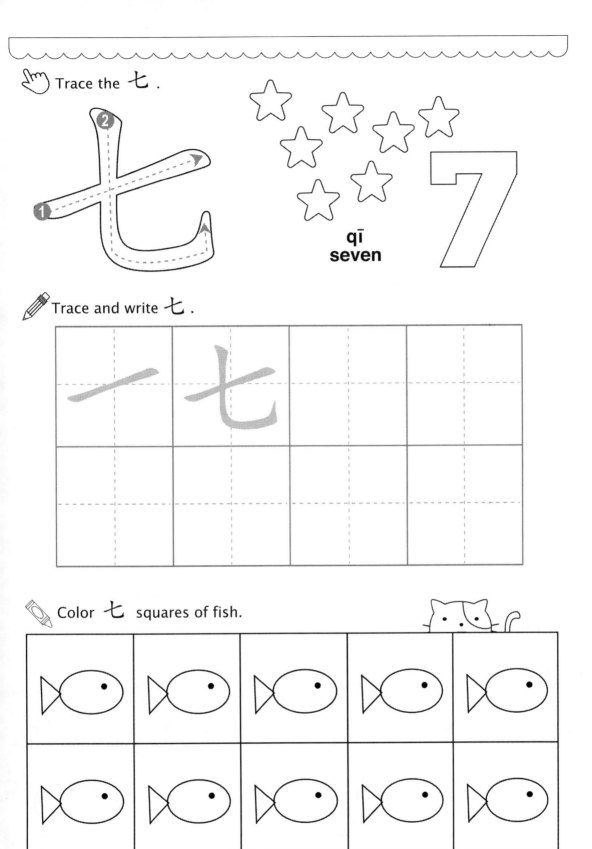

Trace the 七.

qī
seven

Trace and write 七.

Color 七 squares of fish.

Trace the 八 .

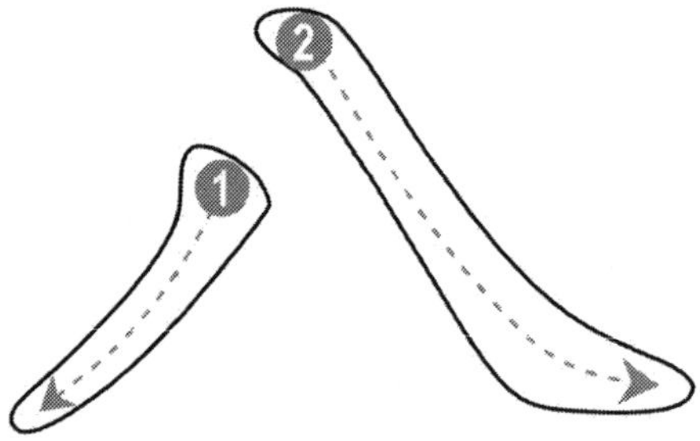

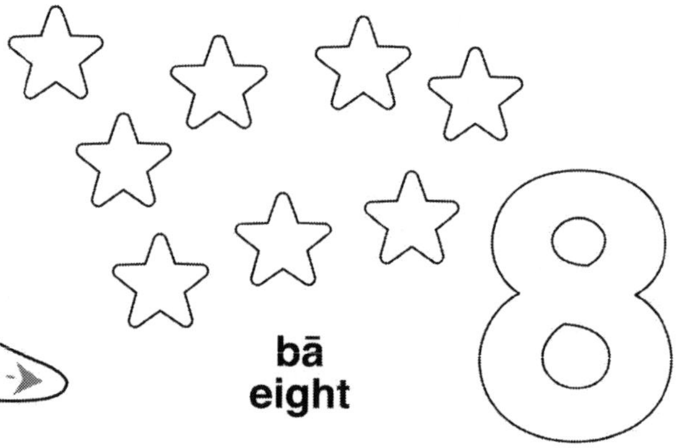

八

bā
eight

8

Trace and write 八 .

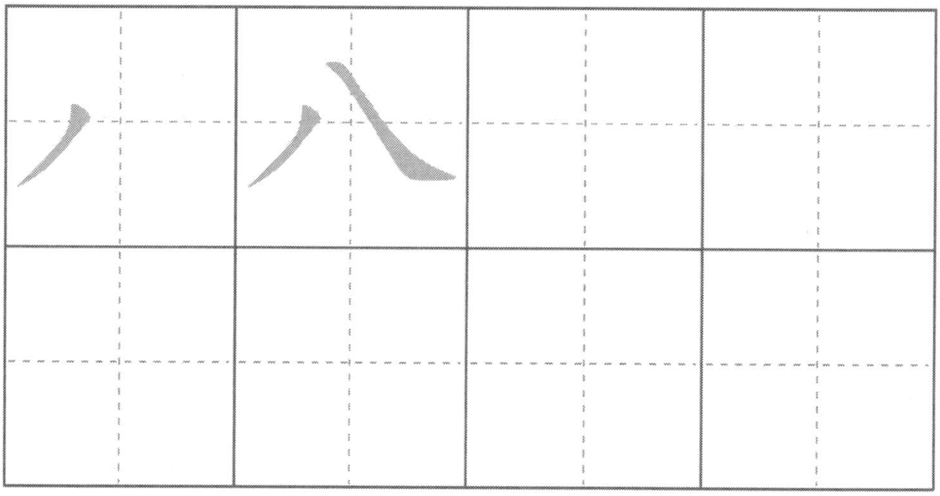

Color 八 squares of fish.

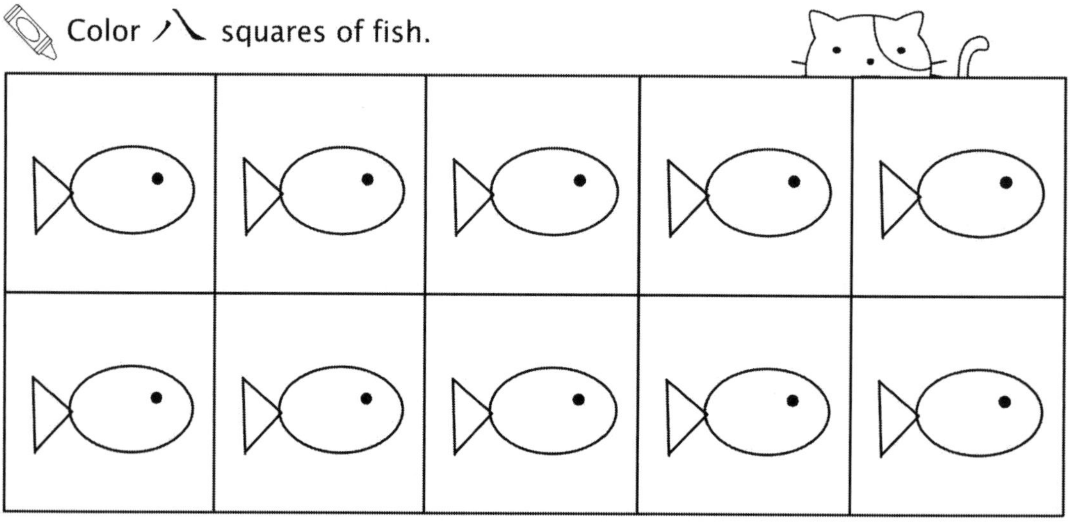

34

Trace the 九 .

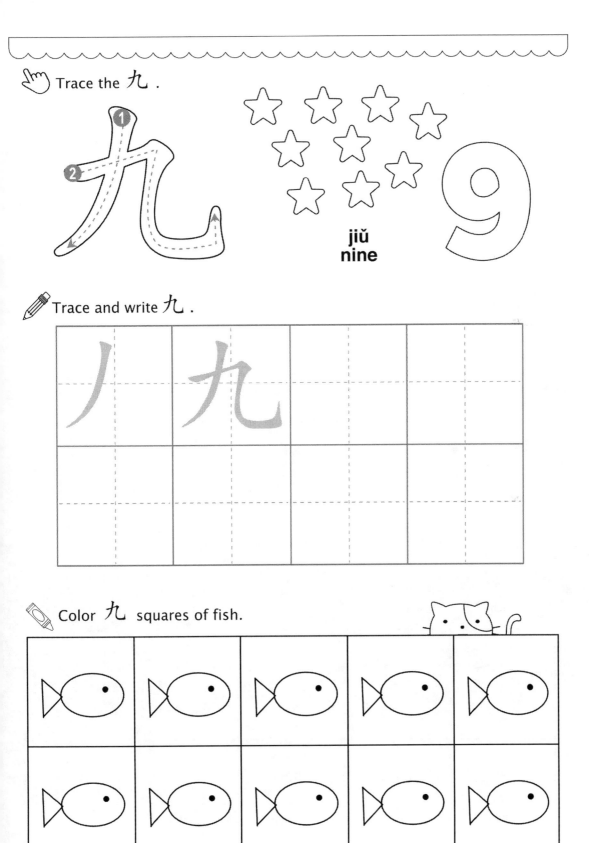

jiǔ
nine

Trace and write 九 .

Color 九 squares of fish.

Trace the 十.

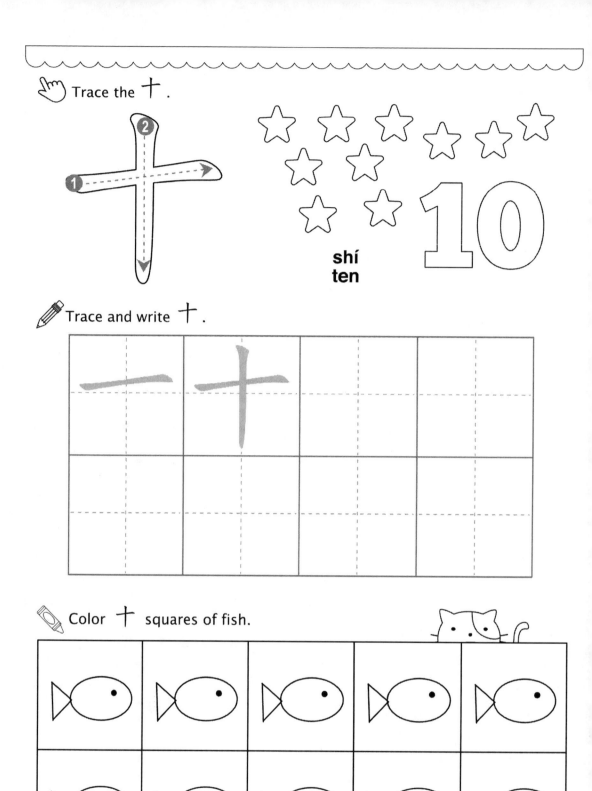

shí
ten

Trace and write 十.

Color 十 squares of fish.

36

Let's Review Numbers 1-10

✎ Follow the numbers to help the big fish find the small fish.

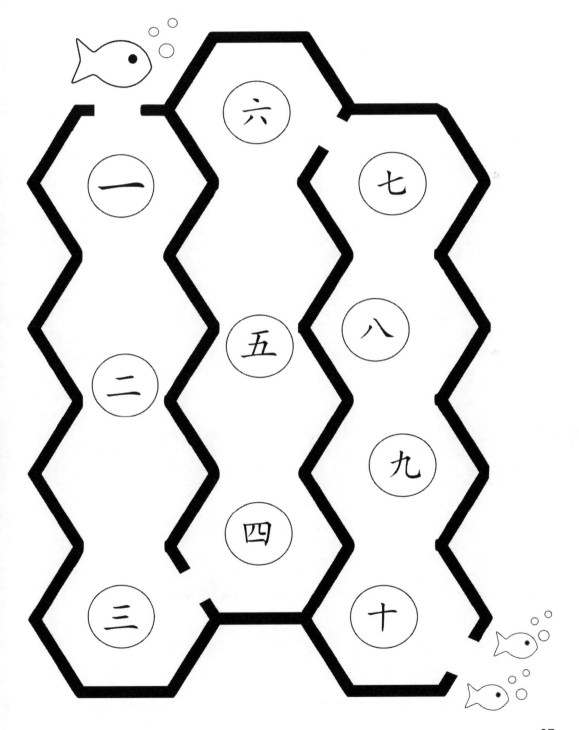

Let's Review Numbers 1-10

 Write how many fish using numbers in Chinese.

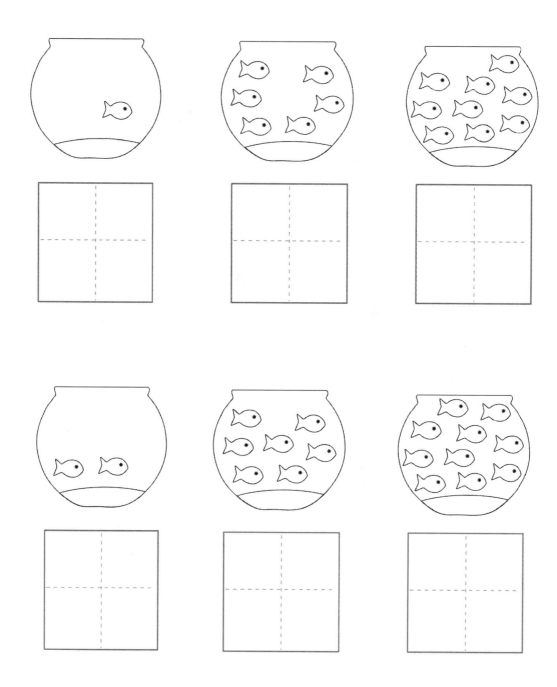

Let's Learn Math Concepts

 There are two characters for the number "2" in Chinese. Let's learn some of the ways to use 二 (èr) or 两 (liǎng).

二
(èr)

两
(liǎng)

Position in a list or group (sequence)

第一 第二 第三

dì yī — first

dì èr — second

dì sān — third

Counting one item at a time

一 二 三

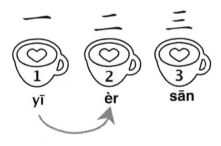

yī   èr   sān

Small numbers

2 → 二 (èr)

12 → 十二 (shí èr)

20 → 二十 (èr shí)

22 → 二十二 (èr shí èr)

Group of two items (except for a pair of items)

 两天

liǎng tiān
two days

Use with measure word or noun (not for "pair" such as a "a pair of hands")

 两个人

liǎng gè rén
two people

两杯

liǎng bēi
two cups

Large numbers

200 → 两百 (liǎng bǎi)

2,000 → 两千 (liǎng qiān)

20,000 → 两万 (liǎng wàn)

👆 Trace each stroke.

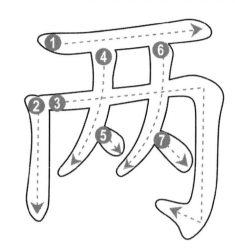

liǎng
two

✏️ Trace and write 两 .

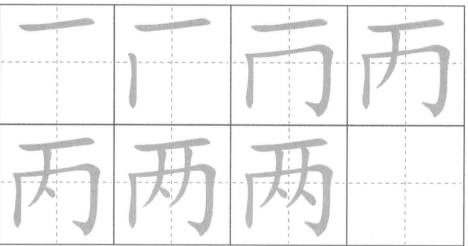

🖍️ Color 两杯 liǎng bēi (two cups).

Let's Review 二 and 两

 Circle 二 or 两 .

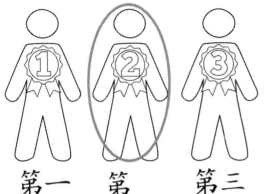

第一　　第　　第三
dì yī　　dì ___　　dì sān
first　　　　　　　third

二　　两

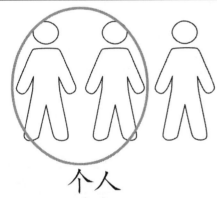

___ 个人
___ gè rén
___people

二　　两

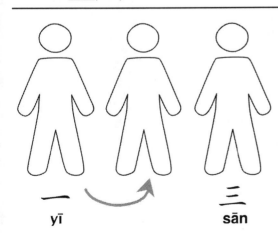

一　　　　　三
yī　　　　　sān

二　　两

41

Let's Learn Measure Words

 A measure word is used between a number and noun (person, animal, place or thing) to show one or more of that noun. Let's look at one way of how a measure word is used.

| how many | measure word | noun |

⬇

| 三
sān
three | 个
gè | 月
yuè
month |

⬇

三个月
sān gè yuè
three months

 There are many different measure words. The meaning of the noun will help tell you what measure word is best. Let's look at some measure words.

Measure Word	When to Use	how many / measure word / noun
个 gè	for people, general purpose, for nouns that do not have their own specific measure word	一个人 yī gè rén one person
只 zhī	for most animals (except large animals or those with long and flexible bodies)	两只羊 liǎng zhī yáng two sheep
本 běn	for books, magazines or notebooks	三本书 sān běn shū three books

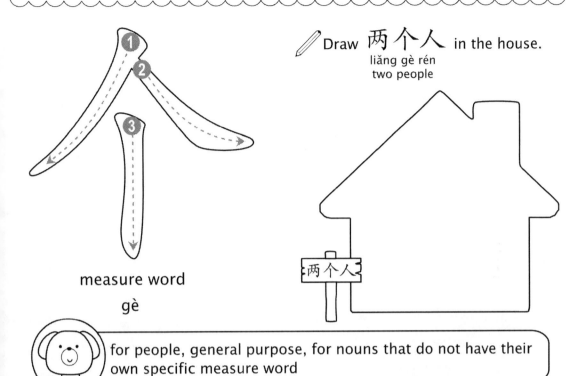

✏️ Draw 两个人 in the house.
liǎng gè rén
two people

两个人

measure word

gè

for people, general purpose, for nouns that do not have their own specific measure word

✏️ Trace and write.

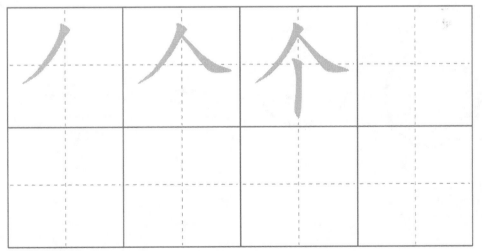

 Color each block with a measure word in it.

八 〉 个 〉 月

bā gè yuè
eight months

Fill in the measure word.

sān gè rén
three people

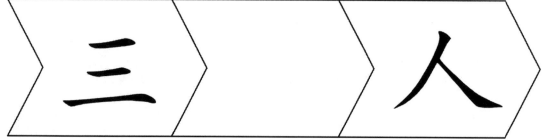

三 〉 〉 人

sì gè qiú
four balls

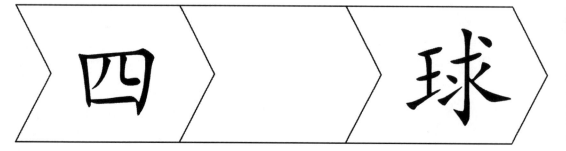

四 〉 〉 球

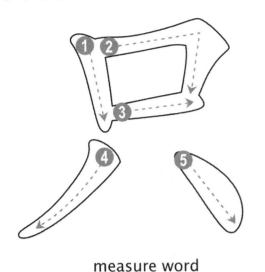

Draw 一只羊 in the field.
yī zhī yáng
one sheep

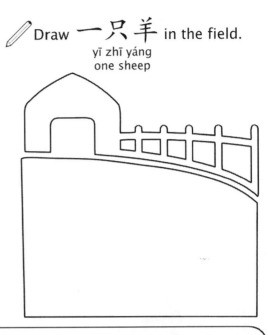

measure word
zhī

 for most animals (except large animals or those with long and flexible bodies)

 Trace and write.

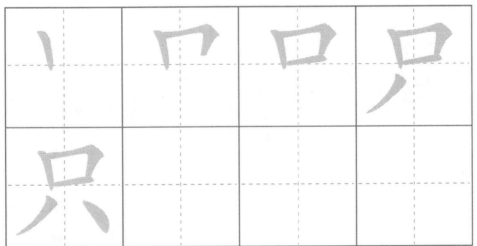

 Color each block with a measure word in it.

sān zhī yáng
three sheep

Fill in the measure word.

wǔ zhī yáng
five sheep

五 > > 羊

yī zhī shǒu
one hand

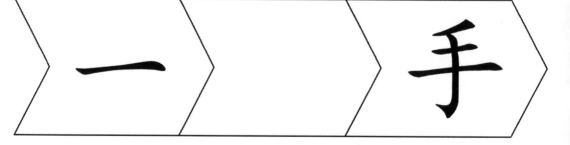

一 > > 手

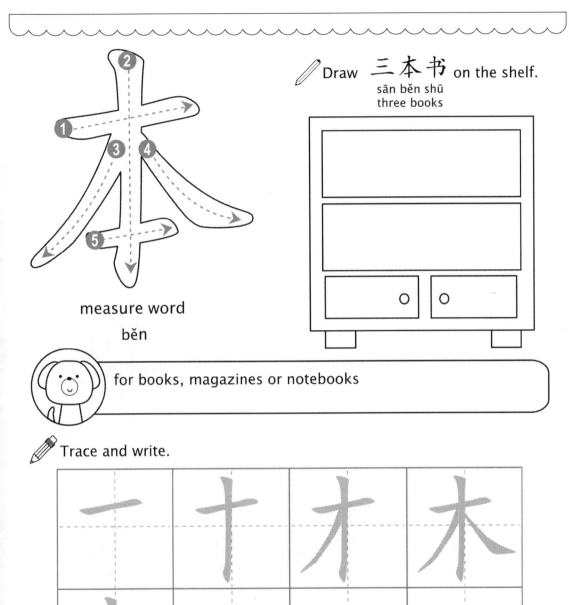

measure word

běn

✏️ Draw 三本书 on the shelf.
sān běn shū
three books

for books, magazines or notebooks

 Trace and write.

一 十 才 木

本

🖍️ Color each block with a measure word in it.

shí běn shū
ten books

Fill in the measure word.

 Count and color the correct number of books.

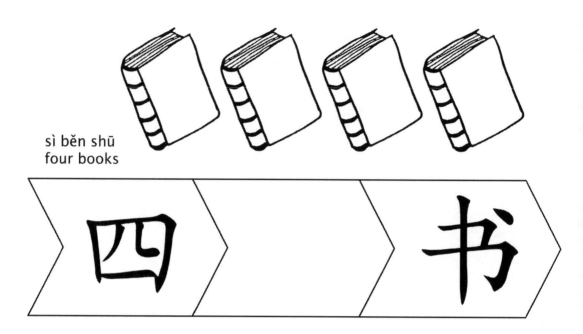

sì běn shū
four books

四 书

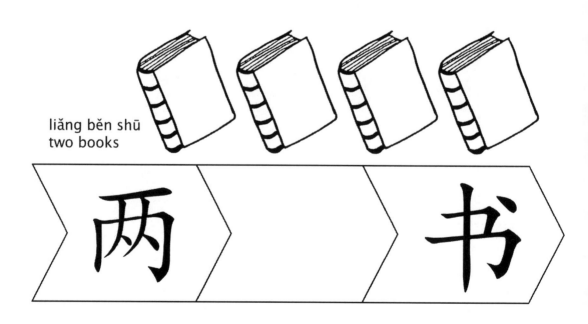

liǎng běn shū
two books

两 书

Let's Learn Measure Words

Some nouns can be measure words too. Let's look at the noun below.

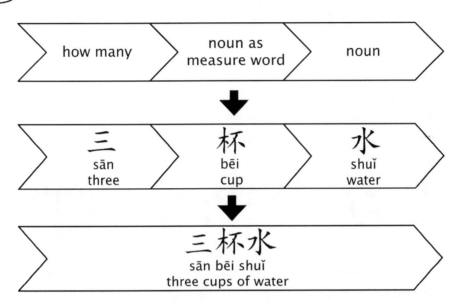

| how many | noun as measure word | noun |

三	杯	水
sān	bēi	shuǐ
three	cup	water

三杯水
sān bēi shuǐ
three cups of water

A few nouns do not need a measure word to show how many. Let's look at the noun below.

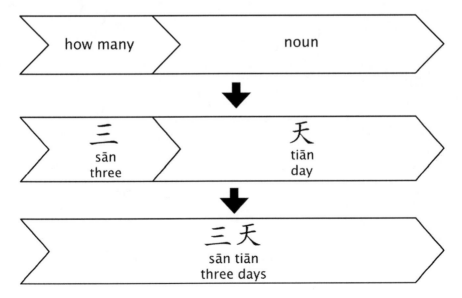

| how many | noun |

三	天
sān	tiān
three	day

三天
sān tiān
three days

Count and color the correct number of cups.

sì bēi shuǐ
four cups of water

 Count and color the correct number of days.

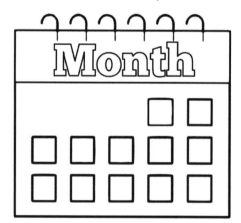

bā tiān
eight days

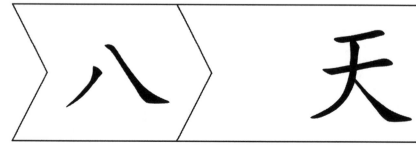

Let's Review Measure Words

 Draw a line to match each picture to a measure word or noun.

Let's Learn Chinese Culture

 In Chinese culture, some numbers are believed to have lucky or unlucky meanings. Let's look at the playing cards below.

 Color each playing card.

三
sān

life   3

六
liù

peace   6

四
sì

bad luck   4

八
bā

wealth   8

九
jiǔ

long life   9

Let's Learn Chinese Culture

✏ Draw a playing card with your favorite number.

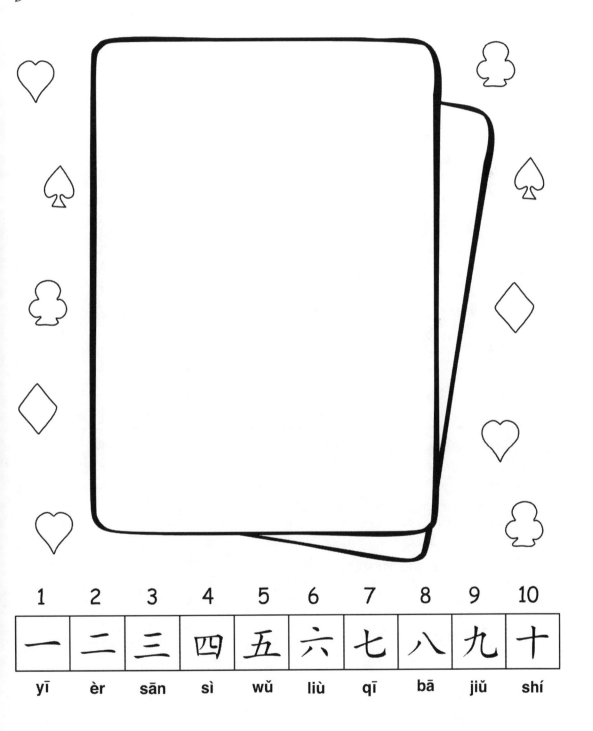

1	2	3	4	5	6	7	8	9	10
一	二	三	四	五	六	七	八	九	十
yī	èr	sān	sì	wǔ	liù	qī	bā	jiǔ	shí

Let's Make A Checklist

Hurray! You have done a great job learning Chinese. Let's see how you feel about what you can do. Learning Chinese takes a lot of practice. Keep up the good work.

Task	I Can Do	I Can Do With Help	This Is A Goal
I can write basic strokes			
I can write compound strokes			
I can match at least one word with its opposite			
I can count numbers from 1 to 10			
I can write numbers from 1 to 10			
I can show someone one example of when to use 二			
I can show someone one example of when to use 两			
I can use at least one measure word to show how many			
I can write my favorite number			
I can learn more			

Trace each stroke.

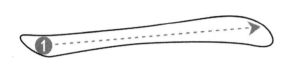

yī
one

 Trace and write.

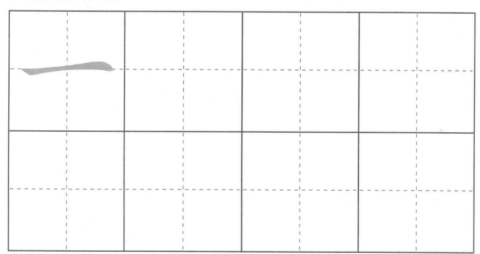

 Trace the character — to make a different number.

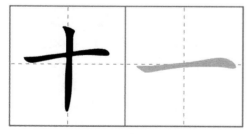

shíyī
eleven

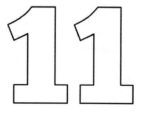

Trace each stroke.

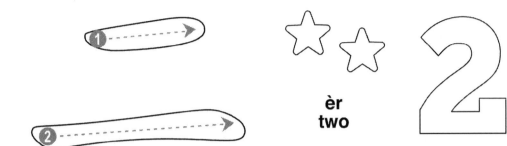

èr
two

Trace and write.

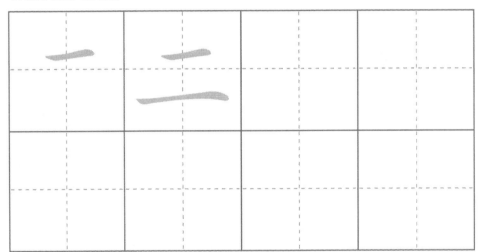

Trace the character 二 to make a different number.

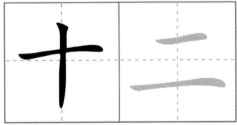

shí'èr
twelve

Trace each stroke.

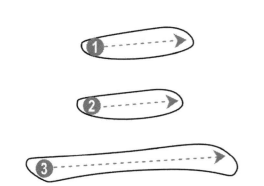

sān
three

 Trace and write.

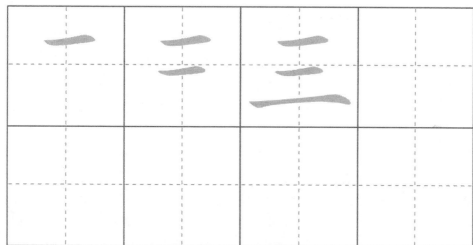

 Trace the character 三 to make a different number.

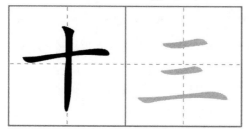

shísān
thirteen

Trace each stroke.

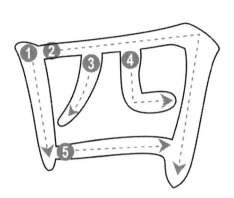

sì
four

 Trace and write.

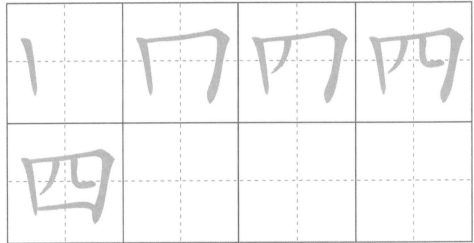

 Trace the character 四 to make a different number.

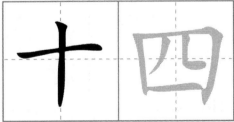

shísì
fourteen

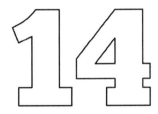

✋ Trace each stroke.

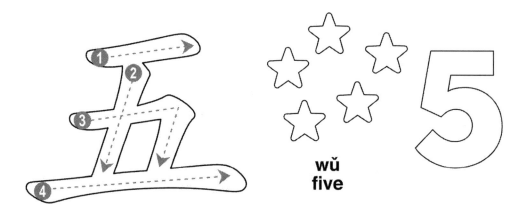

wǔ
five

✏️ Trace and write.

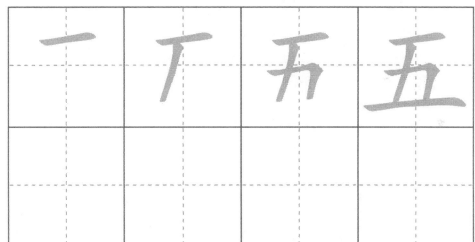

✏️ Trace the character 五 to make a different number.

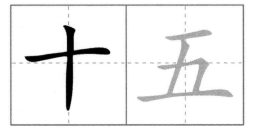

shíwǔ
fifteen

🖐 Trace each stroke.

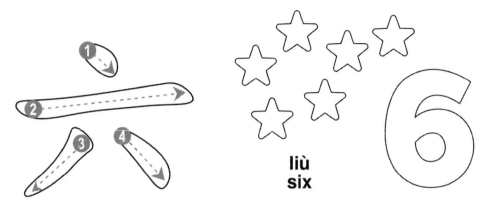

liù
six

✏️ Trace and write.

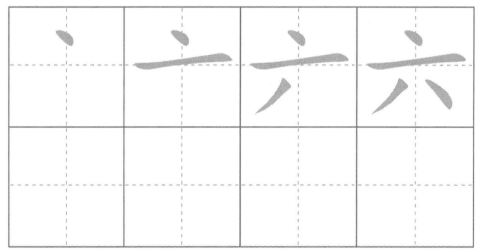

✏️ Trace the character 六 to make a different number.

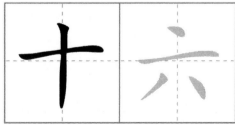

shíliù
sixteen

Trace each stroke.

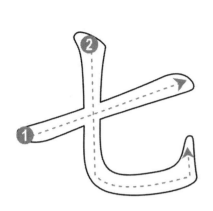

qī
seven

 Trace and write.

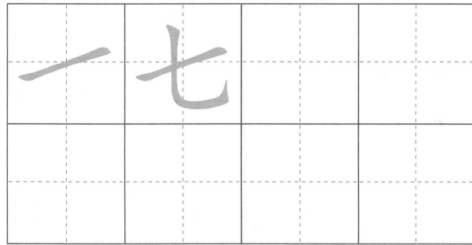

 Trace the character 七 to make a different number.

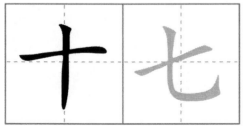

shíqī
seventeen

👆 Trace each stroke.

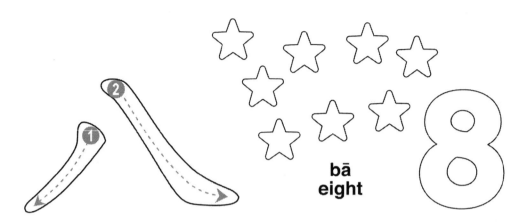

bā
eight

✏️ Trace and write.

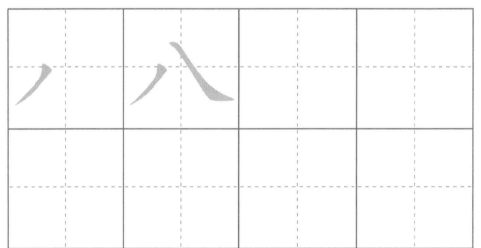

✏️ Trace the character 八 to make a different number.

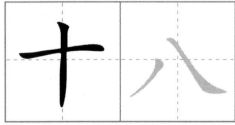

shíbā
eighteen

62

Trace each stroke.

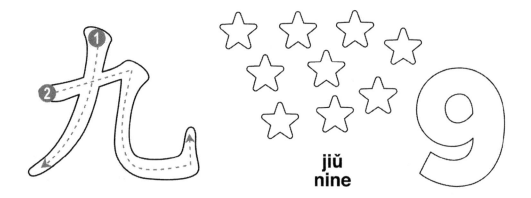

jiǔ
nine

 Trace and write.

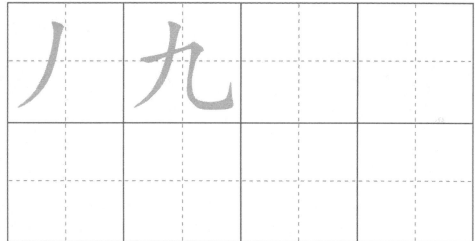

 Trace the character 九 to make a different number.

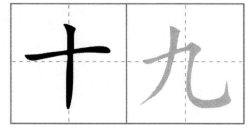

shíjiǔ
nineteen

Trace each stroke.

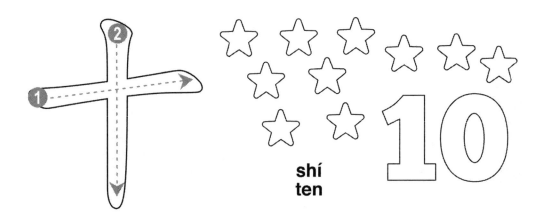

shí
ten

Trace and write.

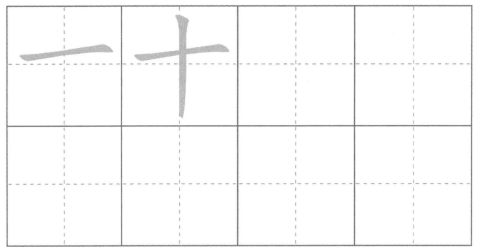

Trace the character 十 to make a different number.

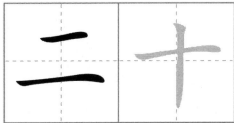

èrshí
twenty

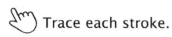 Trace each stroke.

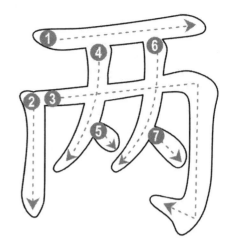

liǎng
two

 Trace and write.

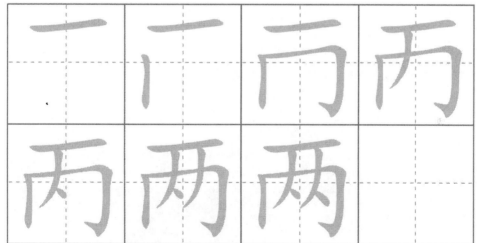

 Trace the character 两 to make a phrase.

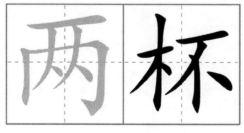

liǎng bēi
two cups

Trace each stroke.

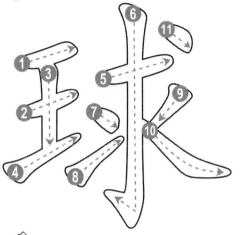

qiú
ball

 Trace and write.

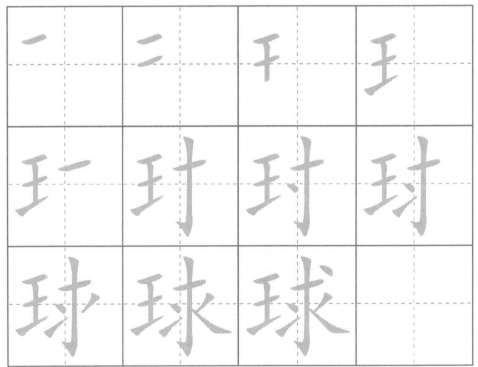

Trace the character 球 to make a word.

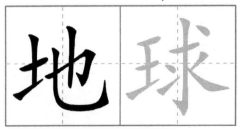

dìqiú
earth

Trace each stroke.

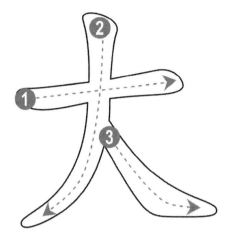

dà
big

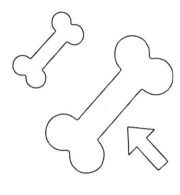

 Trace and write.

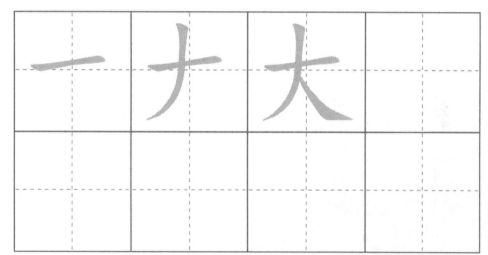

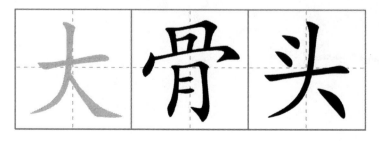 Trace the character 大 to make a phrase.

dà gǔtou
big bone

Trace each stroke.

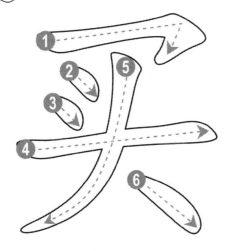

mǎi
buy

 Trace and write.

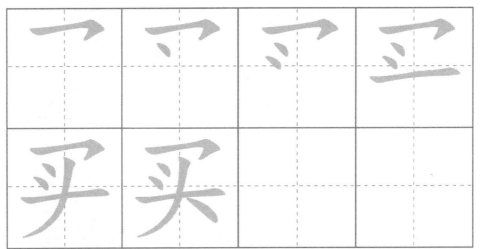

 Trace the character 买 to make a phrase.

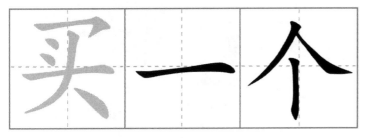

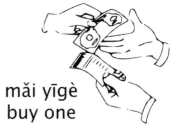

mǎi yīgè
buy one

Trace each stroke.

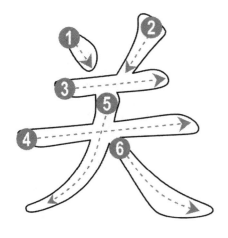

guān
close

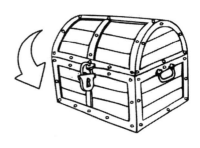

 Trace and write.

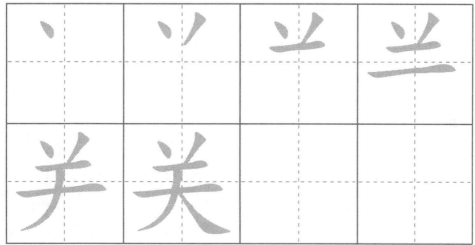

 Trace the character 关 to make a phrase.

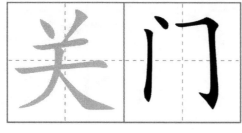

guānmén
close the door

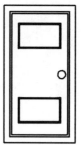

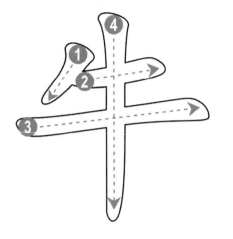 Trace each stroke.

niú
cow

✏️ Trace and write.

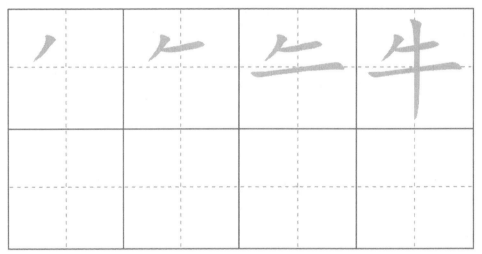

✏️ Trace the character 牛 to make a word.

niúnǎi
milk

Trace each stroke.

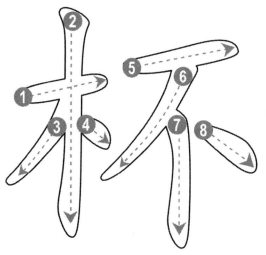

bēi
cup

 Trace and write.

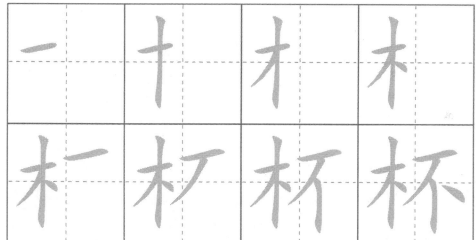

 Trace the character 杯 to make a phrase.

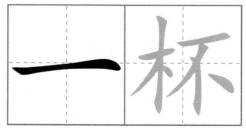

yībēi
one cup

Trace each stroke.

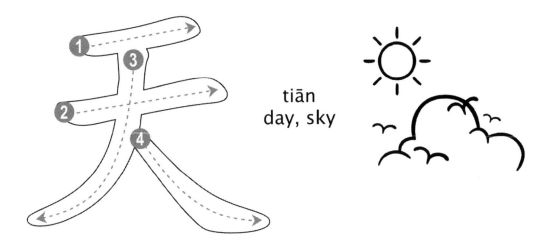

tiān
day, sky

 Trace and write.

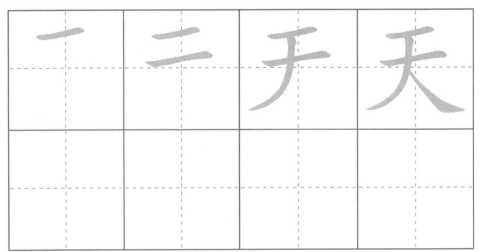

 Trace the character 天 to make a word.

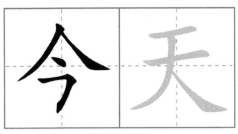

jīntiān
today

Trace each stroke.

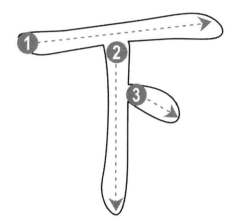

xià
down

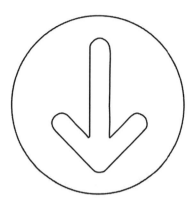

 Trace and write.

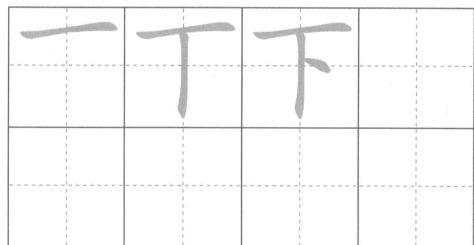

 Trace the character 下 to make a phrase.

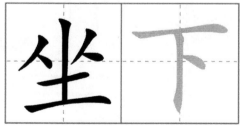

zuò xià
to sit down

👆 Trace each stroke.

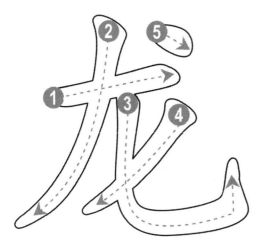

lóng
dragon

✏️ Trace and write.

一	丆	尤	龙
龙			

✏️ Trace the character 龙 to make a phrase.

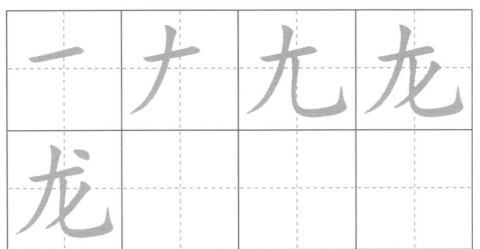

lóngzhōu
dragon boat

Trace each stroke.

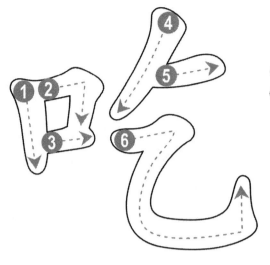

chī
eat

 Trace and write.

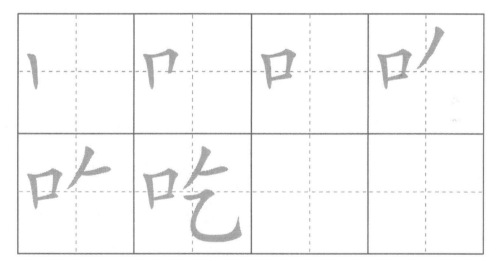

 Trace the character 吃 to make a phrase.

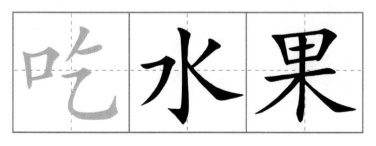

chī shuǐguǒ
eat fruit

👆 Trace each stroke.

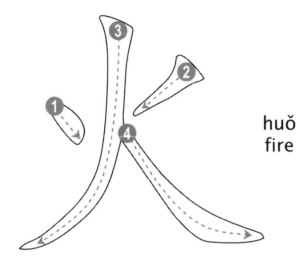

huǒ
fire

✏️ Trace and write.

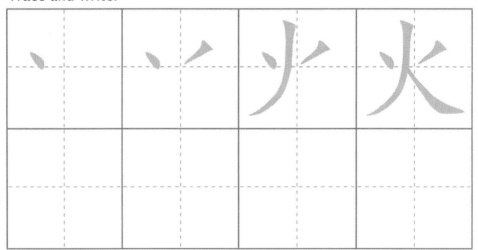

✏️ Trace the character 火 to make a word.

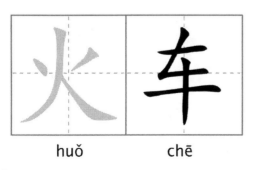

huǒ   chē

huǒ chē
train

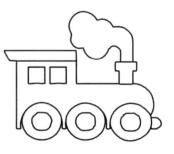

Trace each stroke.

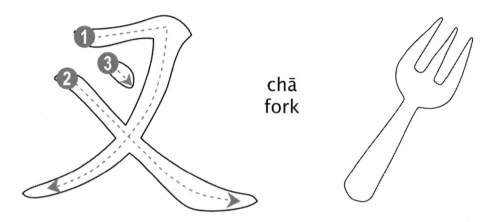

chā
fork

 Trace and write.

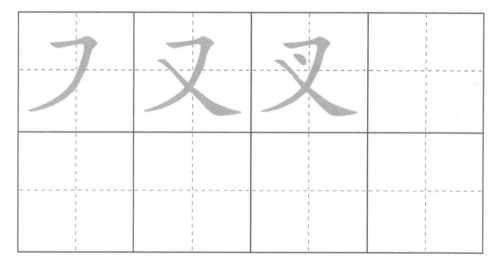

 Trace the character 叉 to make a word.

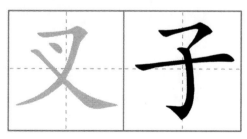

chāzi
fork

Trace each stroke.

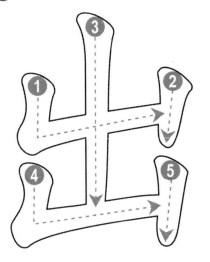

chū
go out

 Trace and write.

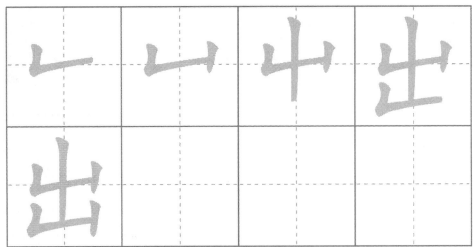

 Trace the character 出 to make a phrase.

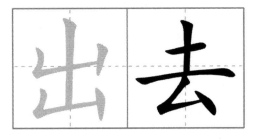

chūqù
go outside

Trace each stroke.

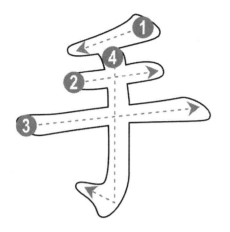

shǒu
hand

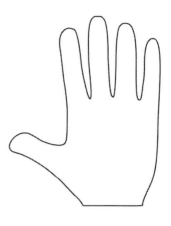

 Trace and write.

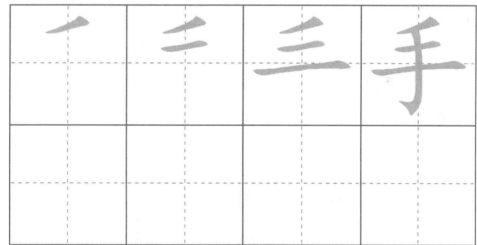

Trace the character 手 to make a phrase.

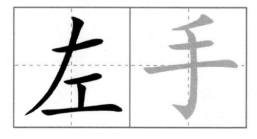

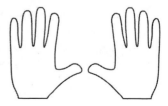

zuǒshǒu
left hand

Trace each stroke.

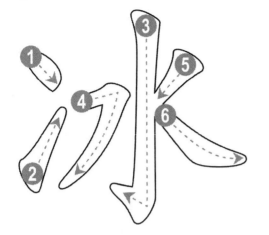

bīng
ice

 Trace and write.

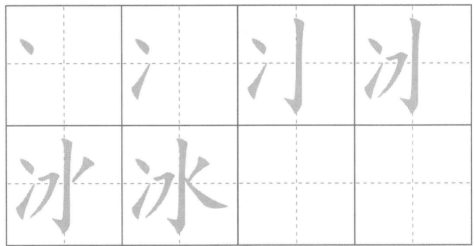

 Trace the character 冰 to make a word.

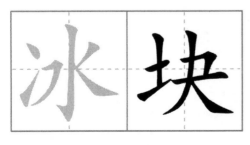

bīng kuài
ice cube

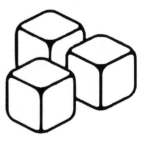

Trace each stroke.

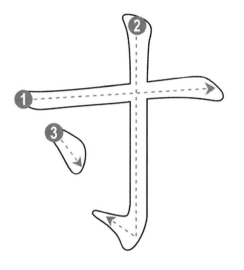

cùn
inch

 Trace and write.

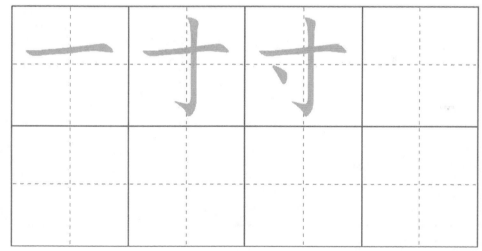

Trace the character 寸 to make a phrase.

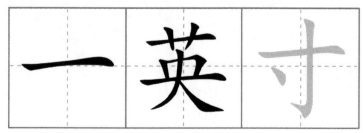

yī yīngcùn
one inch

Trace each stroke.

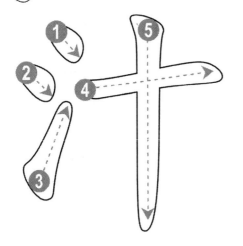

zhī
juice

 Trace and write.

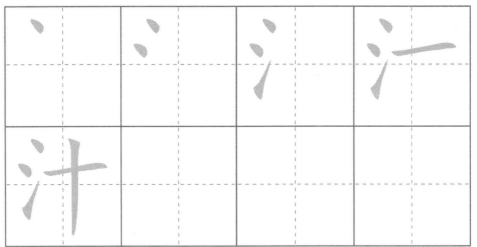

Trace the character 汁 to make a word.

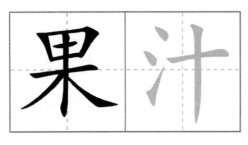

guǒzhī
juice

Trace each stroke.

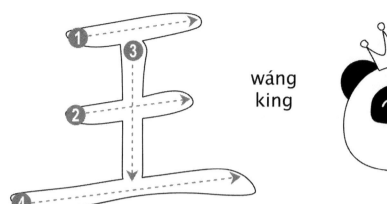 

wáng
king

 Trace and write.

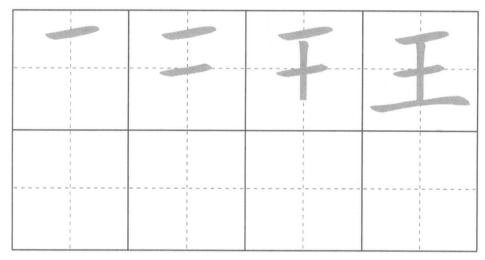

 Trace the character 王 to make a word.

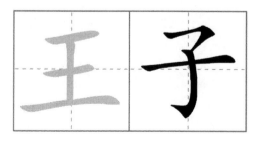

wángzǐ
prince

Trace each stroke.

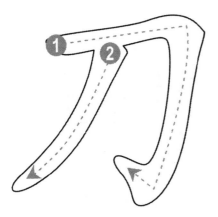

dāo
knife

 Trace and write.

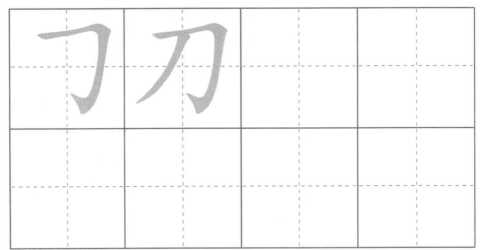

 Trace the character 刀 to make a phrase.

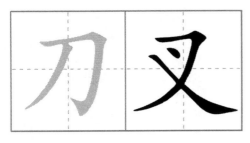

dāo chā
knife and fork

Trace each stroke.

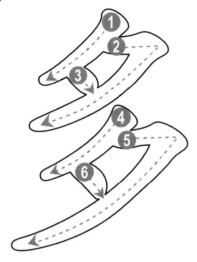

duō
many

 Trace and write.

 Trace the character 多 to make a phrase.

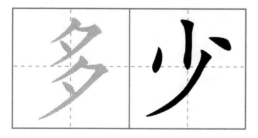

duōshǎo
how many

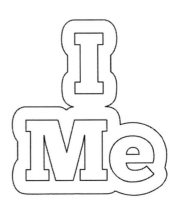

👆 Trace each stroke.

wǒ
I, me

✏️ Trace and write.

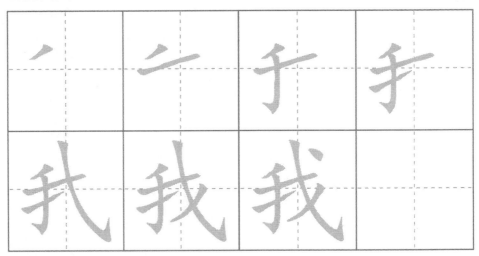

✏️ Trace the character 我 to make a phrase.

wǒ de shū
my book

Trace each stroke.

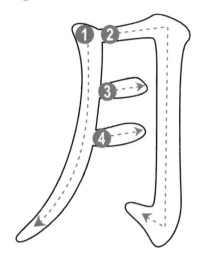

yuè
month

 Trace and write.

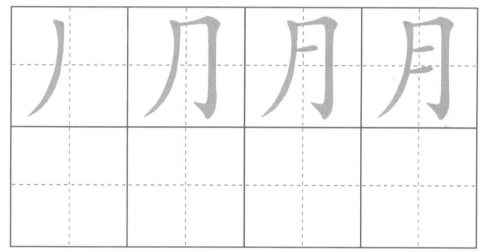

Trace the character 月 to make a word.

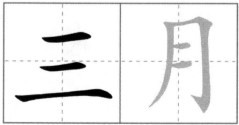

sān yuè
March

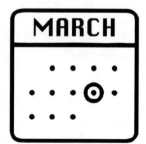

Trace each stroke.

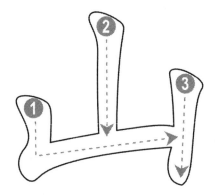

shān
mountain

 Trace and write.

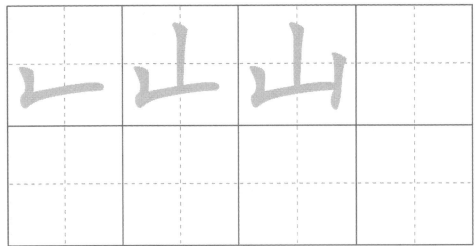

 Trace the character 山 to make a phrase.

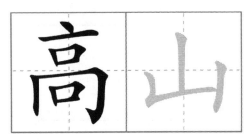

gāoshān
tall mountain

Trace each stroke.

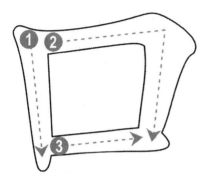

kǒu
mouth

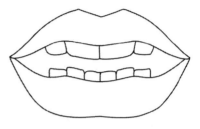

 Trace and write.

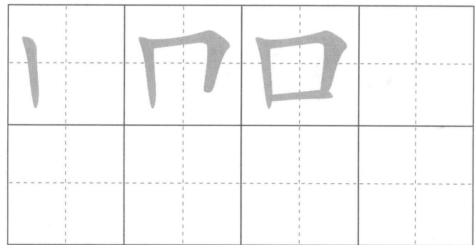

 Trace the character 口 to make a word.

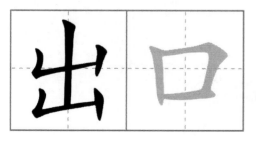

chūkǒu
exit

Trace each stroke.

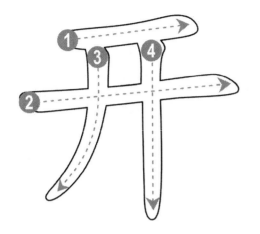

kāi
open

 Trace and write.

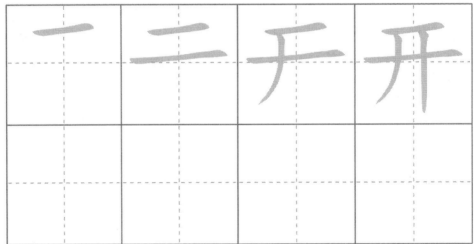

 Trace the character 开 to make a phrase.

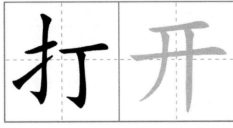

dǎkāi
to open

Trace each stroke.

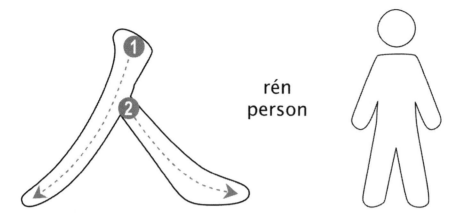

rén
person

 Trace and write.

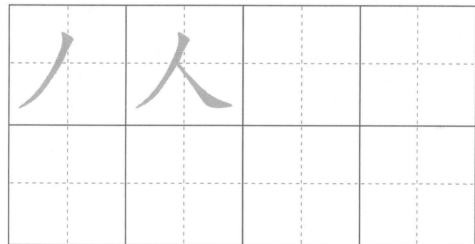

 Trace the character 人 to make a word.

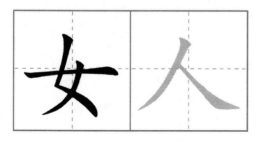

nǚrén
woman

Trace each stroke.

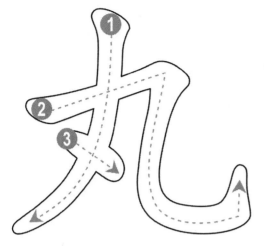

wán
pill

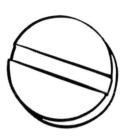

 Trace and write.

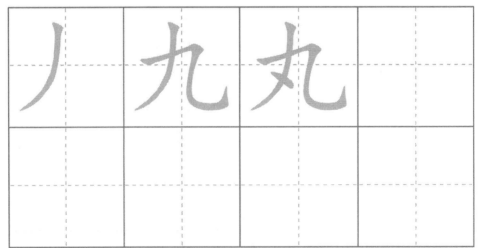

 Trace the character 丸 to make a phrase.

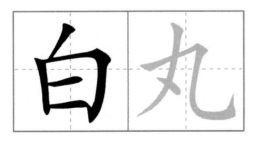

báiwán
white pill

Trace each stroke.

chí
pond

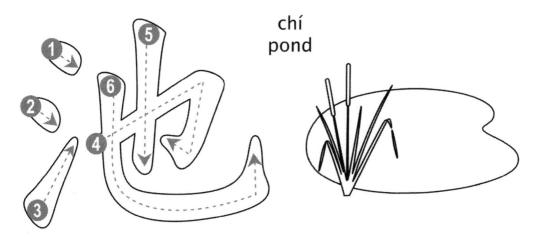

 Trace and write.

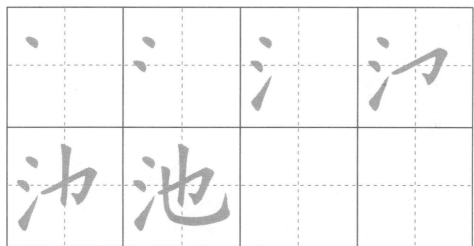

 Trace the character 池 to make a word.

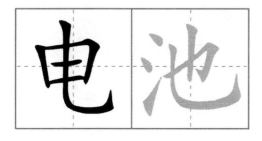

diànchí
battery

Trace each stroke.

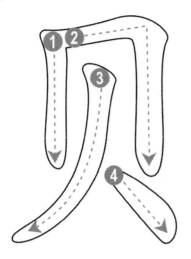

bèi
shell

 Trace and write.

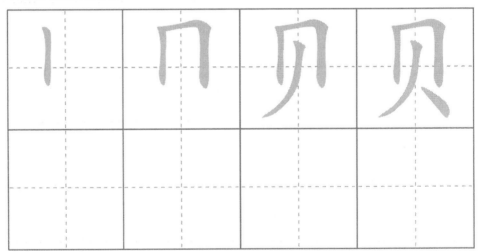

 Trace the character 贝 to make a word.

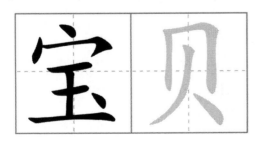

bǎobèi
baby

Trace each stroke.

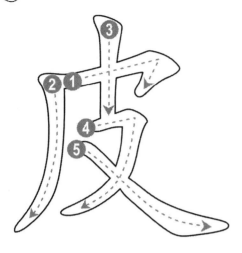

pí
skin

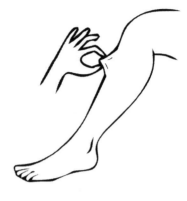

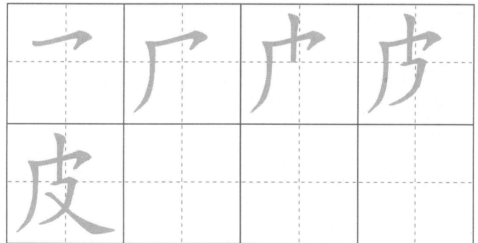 Trace and write.

Trace the character 皮 to make a word.

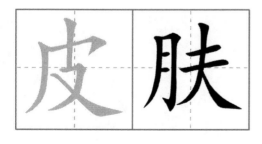

pífū
skin

Trace each stroke.

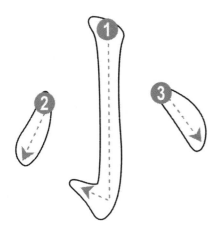

xiǎo
small

 Trace and write.

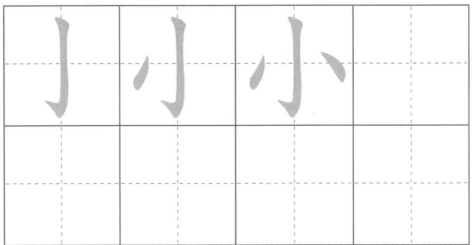

Trace the character 小 to make a phrase.

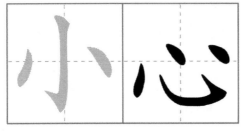

xiǎoxīn
be careful

Trace each stroke.

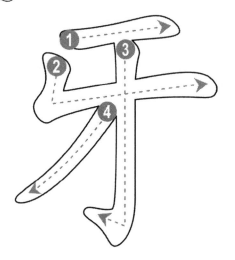

yá
tooth

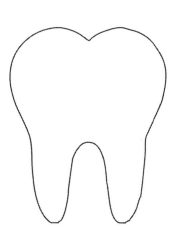

 Trace and write.

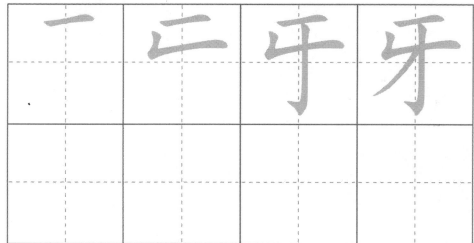

 Trace the character 牙 to make a word.

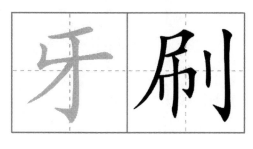

yáshuā
toothbrush

Trace each stroke.

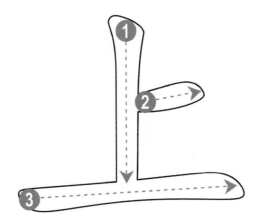

shàng
up

 Trace and write.

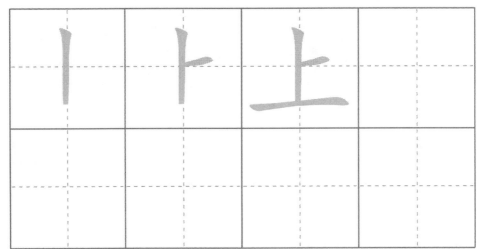

Trace the character 上 to make a phrase.

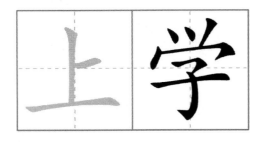

shàngxué
go to school

Trace each stroke.

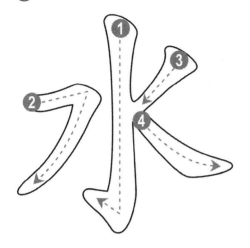

shuǐ
water

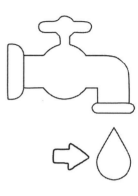

 Trace and write.

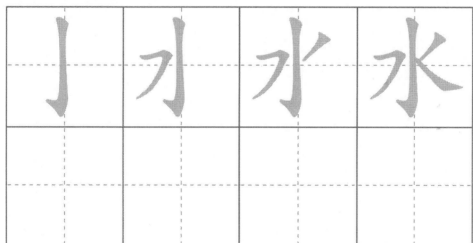

 Trace the character 水 to make a phrase.

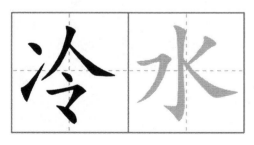

lěngshuǐ
cold water

99

Trace each stroke.

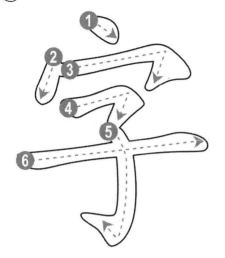

zì
word

 Trace and write.

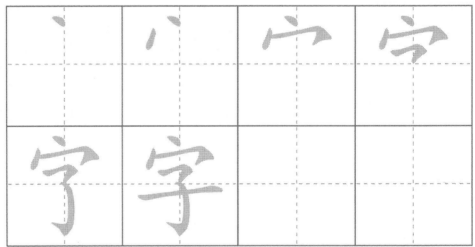

 Trace the character 字 to make a phrase.

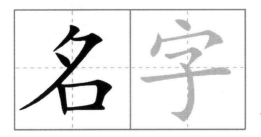

First Name

míngzì
first name

Trace each stroke.

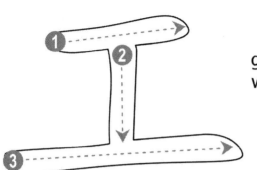

gōng
work

 Trace and write.

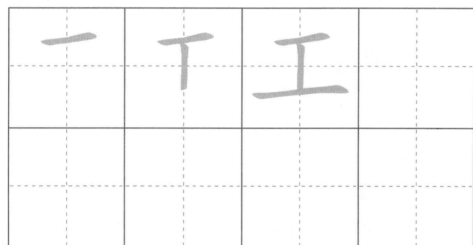

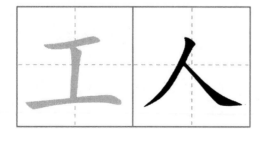 Trace the character 工 to make a word.

gōngrén
worker

Answer Key

Let's Learn Basic Writing Strokes

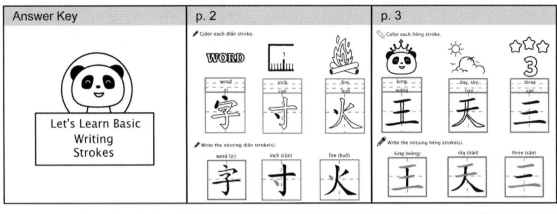

p. 2

Color each diǎn stroke.

word (zì)	inch (cùn)	fire (huǒ)
字	寸	火

Write the missing diǎn stroke(s).

word (zì)	inch (cùn)	fire (huǒ)
字	寸	火

p. 3

Color each héng stroke.

king (wáng)	day, sky (tiān)	three (sān)
王	天	三

Write the missing héng stroke(s).

king (wáng)	sky (tiān)	three (sān)
王	天	三

p. 4

Color each shù stroke.

work (gōng)	ten (shí)	up (shàng)
工	十	上

Write the missing shù stroke(s).

work (gōng)	ten (èr)	up (shàng)
工	十	上

p. 5

Color each piě stroke.

knife (dāo)	big (dà)	hand (shǒu)	cow (niú)
刀	大	手	牛

Write the missing piě stroke(s).

knife (dāo)	big (dà)	hand (shǒu)	cow (niú)
刀	大	手	牛

p. 6

Color each nà stroke.

eight (bā)	person (rén)	fork (chā)
八	人	叉

Write the missing nà stroke(s).

eight (bā)	person (rén)	fork (chā)
八	人	叉

p. 7

Color each tí stroke.

juice (zhī)	ice (bīng)	I, me (wǒ)
汁	冰	我

Write the missing tí stroke(s).

eight (bā)	person (rén)	fork (chā)
汁	冰	我

p. 8

Color each gōu stroke.

water (shuǐ)	small (xiǎo)	inch (cùn)
水	小	寸

Write the missing gōu stroke(s).

water (shuǐ)	small (xiǎo)	inch (cùn)
水	小	寸

p. 9

Color each zhé stroke.

mouth (kǒu)	five (wǔ)	shell (bèi)
口	五	贝

Write the missing zhé stroke(s).

mouth (kǒu)	five (wǔ)	shell (bèi)
口	五	贝

p. 10

Let's Review Basic Writing Strokes

Draw a line from each stroke to complete the robot.

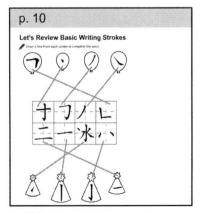

Answer Key

Let's Learn Compound Writing Strokes

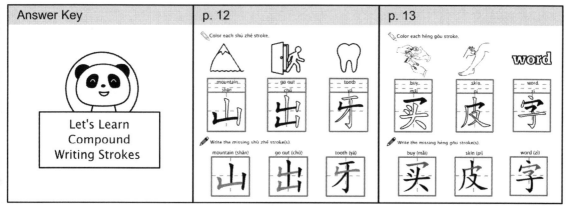

p. 12

Color each shù zhé stroke.

mountain / shān
go out / chū
tooth / yá

Write the missing shù zhé stroke(s).

mountain (shān)   go out (chū)   tooth (yá)
山   出   牙

p. 13

Color each héng gōu stroke.

buy / mǎi
skin / pí
word / zì

Write the missing héng gōu stroke(s).

buy (mǎi)   skin (pí)   word (zì)
买   皮   字

p. 14

Color each héngpiě stroke.

fork / chā
many / duō
water / shuǐ

Write the missing héngpiě stroke(s).

fork (chā)   many (duō)   water (shuǐ)
叉   多   水

p. 15

Color each héng zhé wān gōu stroke.

nine / jiǔ
eat / chī
pill / wán

Write the missing héng zhé wān gōu stroke(s).

nine (jiǔ)   eat (chī)   pill (wán)
九   吃   丸

p. 16

Color each shù wān gōu stroke.

seven / qī
dragon / lóng
pond / chí

Write the missing shù wān gōu stroke(s).

seven (qī)   dragon (lóng)   pond (chí)
七   龙   池

p. 17

Let's Review Compound Writing Strokes

Draw a line from each stroke to complete the word.

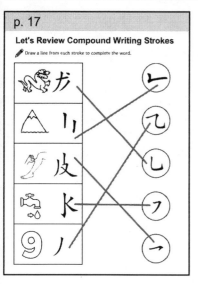

Answer Key	p. 19	p. 20

Answer Key

Let's Learn
Opposites

p. 19

✎ Color the picture that shows 上.

p. 20

✎ Color the picture that shows 下.

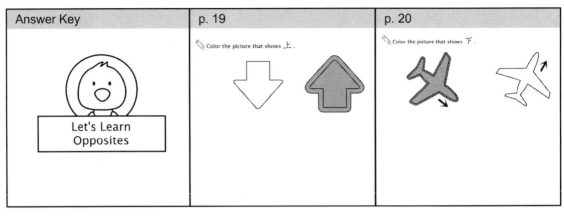

p. 21	p. 22	p. 23

p. 21

✎ Color the picture that shows 大.

p. 22

✎ Color the picture that shows 小.

p. 23

✎ Color the picture that shows 开.

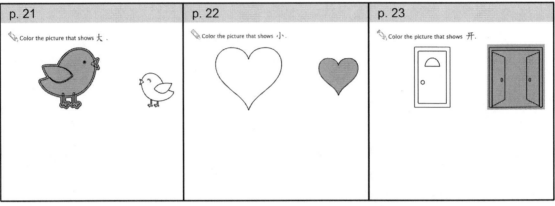

p. 24

✎ Color the picture that shows 关.

p. 25

Let's Review Opposite Words

✏ Draw lines to match the opposite words.

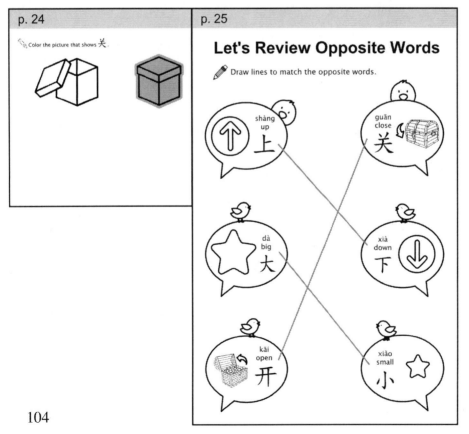

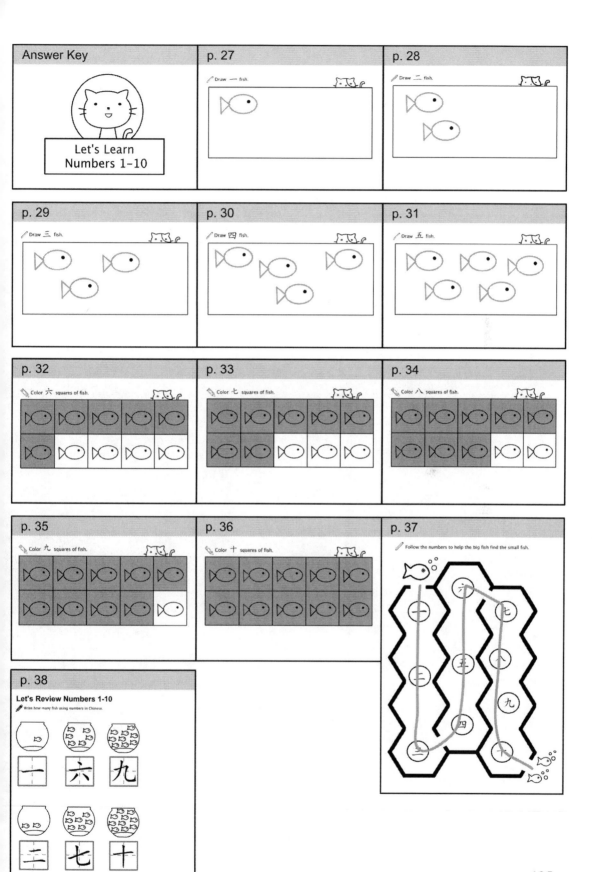

Answer Key	p. 40	p. 41

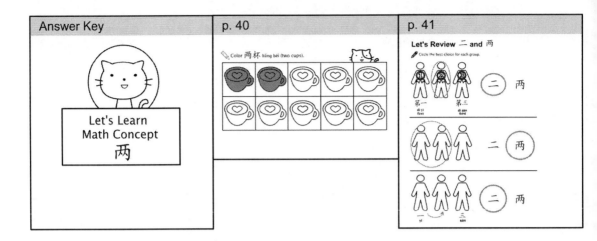

Answer Key

Let's Learn
Math Concept
两

p. 40

Color 两杯 liǎng bēi (two cups).

p. 41

Let's Review 二 and 两

Circle the best choice for each group.

第一 dì yī first   第三 dì sān third   二   (两)

(二)   两

一 yī   三 sān   (二)   两

106

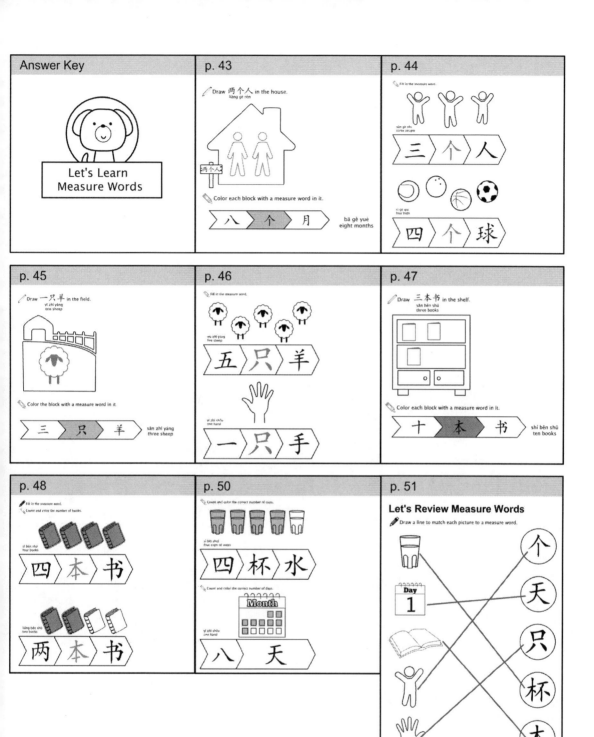

Answer Key

Let's Learn
Measure Words

p. 43

Draw 两个人 in the house.
liǎng gè rén

Color each block with a measure word in it.

八 | 个 | 月

bā gè yuè
eight months

p. 44

Fill in the measure word.

sān gè rén
three people

三 | 个 | 人

sì gè qiú
four balls

四 | 个 | 球

p. 45

Draw 一只羊 in the field.
yì zhī yáng
one sheep

Color the block with a measure word in it.

三 | 只 | 羊

sān zhī yáng
three sheep

p. 46

Fill in the measure word.

wǔ zhī yáng
five sheep

五 | 只 | 羊

yì zhī shǒu
one hand

一 | 只 | 手

p. 47

Draw 三本书 in the shelf.
sān běn shū
three books

Color each block with a measure word in it.

十 | 本 | 书

shí běn shū
ten books

p. 48

Fill in the measure word.
Count and color the number of books.

sì běn shū
four books

四 | 本 | 书

liǎng běn shū
two books

两 | 本 | 书

p. 50

Count and color the correct number of cups.

sì bēi shuǐ
four cups of water

四 | 杯 | 水

Count and color the correct number of days.

yì zhī shǒu
one hand

八 | 天

p. 51

Let's Review Measure Words

Draw a line to match each picture to a measure word.

个
天
只
杯
本

107

Made in the USA
Las Vegas, NV
29 October 2023

79901689R10061